JOKES

Keston Sutherland

JOKES

The Last Books

Love learns by laughing first to speak,
Then slyly gains cares passing great. Fa la.
But I will laugh without that care,
And bid Love touch me if he dare. Fa la.

Mox ubi ridendas inclusit pagina partes,
e vos es leu que·ns gites a carnage. Fa la.
i derisi sogni rinnovellando
on deope sæthe on durelease huse. Fa la.

What is it this time, says the manager. Now look at you, says the dog. Is it that time already, says the pig. Look me in the eye, says the thaumatopsyllus paradoxus, and tell me that you don't know what I mean. Not now, says the manager, I'm expecting to do something else. Give it to me. Give me that break. Says the, says the, how many times do we, give it. Or else. Straight, says the seal. A rest. Here, says. Let's try. You do that. Stupet novo captus, says the hoarse-echoing. Humanitarians on site. Littleneck, carmine ianitor. Says the shepherdless oarfish. That again, shall. Not you again. Baith day. Tergeminus, says the egret, minus the odd captivity. No, it's fine, you go. We, says the tree. And. Frog. Says. Back up a second, says the dog, do I understand. I know. You right. Nycht, says the harp. Take it. Seal. The crackhead haddock, before you jump down my throat. You know where the door is, says the manager, if you don't. Safe. Bring. All I'm saying is. Feeding time, says. Ous of þis loþe. Passage. Is real. Hous. The iniquitous nene. Nextlifelike. What do you mean, says the pig. Vex and smite. That didn't go so well, says the manager, did it, let's start again shall we, everyone count to ten. Eggs. Oh come. Squabs. Vivace spieghi dorate e. A. Mini. Oh come. Nobody. Ye. The food here. I told you once. I already. Nor in the vasty round of this terrene hast thou a friend to set thee free, says the little beewolf, why is that I wonder. Don't look at me, says the giant penguin.

Said. Ate. Isn't great. Is leaving. Ate l'ale. There's no atmosphere, says the boar, everyone is on. Thy will be done. Up on. You had to eat. Fire. Dreariness and coke. Staring at their phones. Look don't touch. Before. It. My time. Five. Lick up all that. If you didn't. Are round. If you don't. Don't. Not now, either, says. Like it. The manager. I don't like it. Like it, says the manager, or lump it. Take it. About us, as the ox. You know what. Sussurratrice. Touch me. Say my. You can. Toucan. Licketh up. Profane me, says the seedy sea wasp, I'll scream for help while you repeat my name. Safe word. Bib. Do. The grass. Garrula e mordace. The ass. Snitches. Don't. Of the field. Get. You. It's the law, says the sky. What's up, says the. Quelle humiliation pour eux, says the pig, de se voir ainsi réduits à n'être, not, quelle humiliation pour eux, de ne se voir pas ainsi réduits à. Wait for it, says the mayfly, too long. N'être. But on our sites there are no casualties. Que des bêtes. Nothing wrong with square one, says the ram's horn squid. It's not so bad. Horny cacomixtle. Many sides. Fy Trumpour that did sic ane deid, God would have your guts for garters, if they weren't such a turn-off after all those years of bloating and chronic inflammation, if there were one. What an unpleasant image, says the manager, I'm not going to be able to get that out of my mind. Enfer anticipé, says the lamprey, careful what you say, we've got plenty of time. If you don't believe me, just think about it. That's a lot of crops, says the skink. It is not easy to think about it. Don't come crying to me, says the wicked moth, they too are dust swept into the hoover in the wind, I'm afraid, they'll be ok in there for a bit. I really am. Wind is no joke. Nor interiority. They hate crops. What is hate, says the pig. So they're a bit picky, says the rattled crocodile, what do you want from them. You can talk, says the parrot. So do I, you say, I hate crops. I can't abide them. I can't stand it when I know there're crops there. I'm not lying. I think I want to go now. Are they there, you say, holding your fingers over your eyes, don't tell me. They're not there, says the manager, relax, let me handle this. Listen, we've all had a hard few years, this won't solve anything, put the starving children down, what can I get you. Surprise me, says the dog. They'll be out of your hair in a minute, says the elephant, anyway, no need to go through the rigmarole of putting them down. Seriously, though, they're only children, says the macaque, why even bother. Do you feel like something cheap and nasty to take the whole of the edge off, says the hippo, in one go, like a Shenzhen egg-slice a vapore, because I do. The dog has been running around in crops, all day, like mad, says the pig, till man say stop. Guess who has tender seedlings and random barley cultivars of an unmerchantable quality stuck in his fur, like little small boat bath toys. Stop lying to us, says the snake, they're there, I'm looking at them right now. They're everywhere. I'm not, you. I'm not even here. But there you are, says the batty kangaroo. What do you get if you cross the line with the point. You say. I have to say, for myself, whatever you decide I ought to say, for myself, says the tern, you can't have it all. You're not wrong, says the dace, but you're not having any of what I have to say for myself, I've got hardly any left. I can't move, it hurts, don't make me laugh. Lots of crops, says the bat, are on fire, right now. Open your eyes so they can make it out. Nice try, says the sky, do you think I was born a billion years ago, le ciel voit ce que la terre ignore. Stay still, it won't hurt long. You call that perpetual, you call that orphic. They hate crops, too. So do you.

So do I, you say, I hate crops. Says. I can't stand it when I know there're crops there. Are they there, you say, holding your fingers over your eyes, don't tell me. I'll tell you what, says the sky. Crops, for all their putative unthwartingness, says the lapwing, are one of the main characters in Exodus. Listen, says the mole, they're singing. They're not there, says the manager, leave the blood all over the walls alone, have a chew necklace, what can I get you. Surprise me, says the dog. I'm not surprised, says the pig. I was spitting blood when I found out, says the lamb, I'll be dead soon. The dog, says the pig, has been running around in crops, all day, till man say stop, in boredom and terror, in case he can't stop anything. I heard you the first time, says the gaur, ever I saw your yummy snout. Good tents. He has tender seedlings and random barley cultivars of an unmerchantable quality stuck, like a Wings hit, in his fur. Is anyone actually going to order anything, says the chicken, or are we just going to stand here, chained to the ceiling, with nothing but diapers on, psychotic with dread, in total darkness, listening to the theme from Rawhide, on repeat, at earsplitting volume, for weeks on end. How are we today, says the manager, you're looking preposterous today, wash your hands, sit on my lap, and grab yourself a sniper rifle, quick, before they grow up or starve to death. Do mine, while you're at it, says the lovable gaur, you'd be doing me a favour. Stroke him, if you like, says the lamb, it's ok, he's tame. So am I, you say, I'm tamer than him. I don't bite, watch me. If you don't like the music, says the manager, listen but don't hear. What about the CRC, says the company tortoise. It ill becomes us, says the crane, to complain. It's insane. I can never remember the last time I bit anyone, let alone the last thing, or anything, I never bit. Smell my teeth, if you don't believe me. I hate to break it to you like your mother's neck under a sack of lentils filmed being dropped out of the sky, but speaking as an endangered lifeform myself, you literally just got here, says the springbok, take five. Or one, says the mayfly. You hadn't been you for five minutes before some pig holed up in your head said you're dead, says the dog. It was a lie. Obviously. Not believing it meant you weren't there. Even though you knew damn well you were. Deep down you knew damn well you'd only ever be seconds away from being dead the once, fact, irrespective of your low opinion of seconds, says the pig, you've got no idea. Une dégradation si honteuse est toujours pour eux ce prémier effet de la vangeance divine. Blink and they're all grown up. I like my teeth like I like my crops, on fire in a shelled barn. I hate crops. Leave crops out of it, you say. One day, says the sky, I am going to leave you to it, if you go on. I hatebarley, I hate the diseases of barley, the spots, the chlorotic lesions, the widths of the zones of chlorosis, the sky, the pig, the streaks, the dots, the chlorotic halo, the infected barley stubble, the ascospores, dispersed in the wind and the sleet, the fungal cycle, I hate how it gets everywhere, under your nails, skin and eyelids, barley rash, germ tubes, fractionated bubbles, Benson and Hedges, tridents, like Neptune's trident, but of barley, barley tridents, barley. I hate how everything always gets everywhere. Food doesn't, says the arty-farty eel. Not everywhere. Can I stop you there, says the mad cod. No, you say. I don't get on with crops. I loathe nurse crops. I abhor alfalfa. Nazi crops fuck off. What about hay, says the anchovy. Hay's alright. No, you say, hay is not alright, hay is unspeakable. Okay, says the manager, one thing at a time. No, you say, no things at a time, no hay. Nothing. Can I just say, says the dog, I'm a stray. It hurt. Irrelevant, you say. I hate hay. I hate how it sticks its snout in. I hate how hay is always sticking its snout in all the time. Send them back the lot of them. Who else hates how hay is always sticking its snout in, you say, as if you meant to say it in your head, not out loud, but there was no room, says the dog, or as if you meant to say, stop, go away, or as if you wanted to sing happy birthday, in a doorway, in May, to a sky you skittishly deplore, but can't, not out loud, anyway, because you think you might be listening. Who else hates how hay is always sticking its snout in, you say, not today, on Monday, I hate hay on Monday, nowadays, can't stand it, can't take any more hay, hay out, you may be clever but you don't know what it's like, leave me alone, please go away. I hate hay, sickening bales, bogus forage, thin trees, low pay, shit for provender, hay time, despicable keys, leave me alone, out loud. It's good for cows, says the anchovy. What, you say. What was that you said. I'm just saying, it's different if you're a ruminant. Ah yes, the cow brigade. If they're going to live here they can learn to speak. What, cows, you say, who even cares what they say. What are you saying, says the dog, what are you trying to say, and what does it say about you that you are willing to try. I'm dead, for one, you say. Not like that, says the weasel, use the bucket on the stairs. Anyway, you look fine to me. I am fine, I know. So you said, says the cod, out loud, on a quiet night in in your head, to its other half. I'm going to head in now. When is that, again, says the manager. Now, says your head, now. When do you think. I'm heading up, now, it's getting dark already. No, not now, says your head. Yes, now, says the dog. Listen to you, says the pig. Stay there, I'm on my way. La la I'm not listening. Good luck with that, says the manager, you won't be needing these then. You're not really there, you say, any of you. You're not all there in my head. You're out loud. I'm here, says the lamb, any time you need me, tug the cord. Where are you then. In the hay, on all fours, with a pair of clippers, making eyes, picture me. What hay, where, you say, and when are you there till, and are you okay. I notice you didn't ask about my eyes. That hay, there, right in front of your eyes, in broad daylight, yes I'm fine. It's looking at me now. Are you alone, you say. Not really, I have my television. What day is it there, you say. Pay day, it's always pay day down in the hay. What can I get you, says the manager. Love, says the iguana.

2

Do we have to, says the manager. Ne afyr ðú me fǽle
sprǽce, says the pewit, I'm bursting. A carp, a plate,
a boar, a crocodile, a wall, and a dog walk into a bar,
says. No need, says the tuna. We've come this far, says
the dog, it'd be mad not to. It'd be psychotic not to.
One law, says the pig, for us. One constant day, says
the flesh fly, and all the sun-blushed carrion flower
your heart's content can liquefy. Quite. Nor lessening,
says the orca, nor augmenting. Agony grips. The
great machine no longer rolls, says the calf, you can
come back in now. Lose the chains, says the salp, you
look like the acarewana. They might think you're
taking the piss. Ne lust me wit þe screwen chide, says
the cocky pika, kill the broken lights and open wide.
You mock, says the banana slug, like brain sand in a
lychee, but yet can overbrim the heart. Ivy, get the
mop. Boil me in lead and murder my entire family,
says the manager, if it's not my old managers in arms.
What'll it be. What won't it be, says the hornet. We'll
see. In the flesh, says the pig, as if not available in
spirit. Listen to the prince de froidure, says the catty
alligator, God must be shitting bricks. Big Cypress.
You were ahead of me, says the plate, you go ahead.
It's fine. Spare time, strangle me instead. Outside,
says the manager, it's not raining stones. It's too late
for that. If the cap fits, says the headless nit, like
the pomegranate the planet, or the sky the stars, or
time love, only wear it once and end up throwing it
away. A groper, Sangatte, I get it, kill me now. Kill

me now. E miseri. Where's the landfill in this dive, says the. And, you sneer, mock-inquisitively, who else, while you're at it. Viventi abbandonati, says the tamaraw, get your mouthy ass out of my face, who do you think you are, Balaam. I don't give a rat's heart who put the words in its mouth. Words are important, says the huss. If Balaam's ass had kept its fucking mouth shut we might never have been in this mess. Anyway, who wants another line. When the nut falls. La pieté du lecteur iugera, says the pig, de quelle cöscience proçedent tells illations. Ce pauvre badaud, says the soft-shell crab. I'm not deaf, says the sky, I'm bored, what shall we do. Let swine love husks, says the carp. Hold this, says the stork, I'm going to give that plate that just walked in a piece of my mind. Not in so void here, says is doun þe vemon. The bat. The manager. Languish in my smart, you part. What. Opinion, says the abrenunciated goat, is like a tiny onion. Same again, says the mayfly. Quick. No matter how many layers you peel off, there is never a lot to go. Are you having, says the manager. On another topic, says the shrew, check out the EPS on that. They shall stand upon. Whatever. Bobtail squid. Bobcat. They like. A heap, says. Bobcat. It. Say my name. Don't if you don't. I've. Want to, says the school hare. Got a zip, says the snake, it goes all the way. Eggs, says the hog. Yes, says the manager. How, says the hog, bristling. Any, says the manager, mollificative. Try me. Auch frembde eier. My head. One drinks. All, says the hog. One is fragile, says the badger. Exposed, says the manager. Eggs posed, I. Crushing. Spent. May. Nothing to crush. Hatch'd of. Get it. Truly have the appellative. Deuoutly. Of eggs. Is killing me, says the ostrich, anyone. Into. Th'eggs vnhatch't. Scrambled. Urbane serpent. In the bosom of the womb. A nun's egg. In the egg. Got. To see.

Of. In an. Says. To hatch. Cockatrices. Them. All night. Crack'd. I packed the future. Some. Oöphagy, vanilla. Cavity or. There. Estridge. Emptiness. You. Sunny. Aus. Hedged. Says. At the blunter end. Choice furniture. Hecket. In the. Egg. Dust. With radiant. From my face to the end. Boiled. Heat adust. Unzip me if you. As easily. Like. Massacrously does it. With. Stop. Eggs. Your tongue. Gainst. How do you catch a squirrel, says the limpet, climb a tree and act like a nut. Our Rockes. Every spot on. Egg pie. An egg. Which your foot. Egged. Or a climbing frame. And to bed. Enough. I used to have a job. Why. In a calendar. I got fired. Don't eggs. They'd crack up. Because. Factory. Tell jokes. Because I took a couple of days off.

3

The voice is very weak and open today, and the good
news is brief, I think I am soon about to go out for
a walk, says the mule. Will I go far. Don't crowd
him, says the misunderstood wasp, I'm not here
either, he'll be back. I am back, says the mule. I am
woodness laughing. It never fails, wood man, then
was I. Coming through, says the famished. To. Mind.
Blue. Amaze me. Out. Kangaroo, out. To. Of my.
To. Light. Way. True. Wood wrooþ. Welny wood. Art
wood. Wood. I mean. This place has gone to the dogs,
says the stork. You're out of line, says the manager.
You're not, says the ocelot. Wax ney wod. Step
by. Plot, main, in woodness his chariot. Character.
Motivation. Arc. Wodmen madest. Muzzle velocity.
Plot. Chariot. Gidy and wod. Ongoing genocide.
Sit, let's talk. Says the. Developments. Plot. Crisis.
Resolution. Kangaroo, the wood wyl goo. Pin. Too.
Down your basics. Then build. Stop. Plot. Up sub-
plots. Who's there, tank, tank. The voice is very slow.
Who, says the stork, are you welcome. As he were
wood for wo he gan. Amos. To crye, I am available,
here. Go ahead, Amos. Gentrification, says the. Says
the manager. Everything you have you put into the
grid below for the subplot. Dog, for you. Still, who.
Who. If a man. As well. To go out for a walk, says
the mule. Be braynwode, as the main. Campaign of
political and economic warfare against the United
States. Plot. A mosquito, cool, says the squid. Weird.
Wod. I can't hear myself. Hole. Honk. Think, says

the mole, can everyone. Wodsican. Men. Please just shut the. Stop staring at my. He wold wene. Eyes. Fuck up. I were wod. Wodmen. Rules-based. Then was I wood. Still carrying his aid bag. Wrooþ. No. Wood. I can't hear. Sarah, Sarah. Graveyards. Who. Aloft did steeme. Left. Sa-rah phone I could use. Do þe man þat is frentyk etyn. The sowe freten. Thou, says the mouthy serpiginous. Deep. Deep. In the sheep's buccal. Down you. Mucosa, art. Watch out, says the pig, I think I'm about to throw. Wood. Up. Know. Of an. How. Owle þat howtetz. Rend, it says, their keeper and their leech, it says, says. Hear you do that. Deep down, we are all one. Whitey, says the dog. Breath. Voice. Afraid so, says the pig. I am mensworne. We must not sell it, says the gaur. How, says the trippy floor. Ecce echinatus. No. Cheech, fetch the harrow. There, says. Are we. Cheech. One has his liver overheated, and whoever hears them, bien leitreiz, I mean, says the mule, and I am so alone, since the day my skin was stuffed with walls. Hello, says the mule, what's this. Meant to do. If they wanted to give me something, I would know how to be told to watch out. That. The hells gave their right. He's re-engulfed, says the washed-up skunk, ecce. Bot. Nul. I. Horseshoe toad bat, borderline. Sphagnurus. Quhen ȝe claw. Last night I dreamt I was in a talking. Home. Shop, says the pap. De l'homme. Am. Personality, glaikit. A pack of lies. Ier mâché. Paluster. Þair wame. Wolf. Thay tūmyll. Sun-faded cartons of cereal on chrome wire shelfing, novelties, erasers. Our lyk swyne. Tinned. Dawn of the toad. Is real. Fruit cocktail, everything was talking at once, even the counter. Devant moi. And the sweets. Morir se je l'en. Toad flap. Pooie. Back now. What did it mean, says the cormorant. The mule. I am gooey. I am shooting you dead near the convoy, as you're only trying to feed. Garir. Tapir. I would. Ay woid. It was hard to make out in the dream, I could hear. Take it like a human. All the tongues clicking, but. Over there, says the polar bear, controlling the crowd by fire. Good, says the shrew, boohoo. Clicking, not what they said, but I knew. Like if you. None. I am garish. They were talking, you could sense it. Moved his tongue. Says. Says the pap. The kangaroo. Ier. What can I say, it's the tongue of my dreams, I want to wake up. It is not that by which the tongue is moved. Balaam's ass handed to you. Mâché. Bat, the bathroom scales. Forever hold your. With a grudge against eyesight and a highlighter, says the despicable wren, hunt me, but I have utterly destroyed all that. Please. Just to utter words. Stop. Breathed, says the bar-tailed. Beewolf. Pertinacious godwit. Something, I don't know. Plot. What. Recited some funeral verses. Ecce. By Rückert, Auch meinen Werth hat something something, says the walrus. No need, says the manatee, to whistle while. Odobenus. Beg. So recht. I'm a great believer. Rosmarus rosmarus. Ecce my. Zu. Declaw me. Würdigen ver. Says. In equality. Who says, says. Ass. The koodoo. Or I'll scream. So far as it ever goes. You have changed the centuries of what I saw, says the mule, behold my pia mater, we were still alive overseas, the sorrow he felt toward a fly, a brain, a devoted mother embracing her only child, swatted against a wall. Can you believe it. Orca. Standen. Can you get a replacement hoover bag, if you're going out, says the manager. Noli ergo pia mater spernere. Eggs in hay. A stray word. Me. Gush. New Labour. Labour. Emunim. Cross-legged tick eggs. Korn. Lamashtu. Korn. Expungement requests. And I looked and saw a bloody pit, says the. The sky. Viscid black earth. I'm

not cleaning. Plastered with lungs. Knock, who's. Of
a swine. That up, says. You've made your point, says
the manager. Now drop it.

Men. The feeder being. Porcum. And the feeder. Not only that. Had þe feveres and. Effected the feeder. Debes inversum. Pig. Dog. Egg. I. Bestes þe schyt, says the. Pig. Ponere. Pots. Bring the pawl. To drynke þ morowtid. Egg. Quem per. Rotatable. Dog. Gaga. Zaza. Filling-feeder. By the dog, when. Men. Repeat. Oft wird ganz. Feeder fiend. Zakat. The madness of NPR. Feeder. Forage. It's a mental institution on steroids. Medium. A drum. Lipstick on a pig. Says the pig. Gutturis incides. Dull lager. I like. John Deere. You need water, you need everything. Cut Act. It is happening. Cuffed and blind. They've got so much money, look at them. They've got nothing. Cut off from the waters. But cash. Their husbands are great. Feral Swine. That come down from above. Yekatit is there 12 anywhere, says the flatworm. Eradication Program. In other words, whether or. That's more fun to be. That's. Nice flame cell, says the sleazy llama. Folded. The nicest thing anyone ever said to me, says. More like it. Not, we're going to kill the slug. Cheer up, the manager. Immer. Discharged from the feeder. Protect our herds. And lete him drynke. Ouum, ouiculum, ouulum. Eine. Not my type, says the flatworm, als þe. Don't. By fending off foreign animal diseases. Unhinged. Unwahrheit gesagt. Yholk. A skeleton walks into a bar. Flatter. Broken Abyssinian arrogance. Doggitless. Horse's mouth. Yourself. Ymyddes þe egge. Quick, doggitless, says the nit, I'm still. Stick your fingers in me. All

Nations strive to free themselves as far as. A. Possible from economic dependence on foreign countries. Bit itchy. Lys, and þe white obout on þe same. Of our fear. Nut job. Ne so. Says. Wel can noman affile his tunge. The llama. Dog. That som. It happened, therefore it can happen. Time. Wys, right. Him. Ipsilateral to the stimulated. Scum. Ear. Again. Swa es þe erthe. Radical lunatics. True and fruitful. Peace. Peace. Big beautiful. In the context of them not. Mai som. Tempered. Having. To the hardness of steel. Liht. Inmidst the heavens that. Our own right, always and unflinchingly. I give up, says the pig. Word overscape. Gas. Because it croaks every day, says the. Obout. Off the rails. Nato a. Lobster. Perir. Arm'd in Lobster. Nutrito in pene. Makrels and Lobsters. Incentives. And like. Chicken. Hop, GH, fog, gop, a Lobster boil'd, the Morn. Courting us to the reception of Aliment. Black to red began. F. On-go, onʒon. Moose. Again. Irishry. To turn.

What's that you're reading, you say, no idea, I want to read that, this, you say, oh nothing, I just picked it up, I'm not really reading it, to be honest, go away, I'm trying to read. What with all this noise. Ich bin komen an die stat, dâ got menischlîchen trat. Got pictures. Quite honestly, I don't know what I'm meant. T'eh eeit, t'eh eeit. Hit me, hit me. Proeza grans, proeza grans. You read my mind, says the pronghorn, how do I know you were really reading that either. Have you got to a good bit, says the planktonic crab. They're all good, says the platonic crab. The bit where underage wrestle with error, t'eh eeit, blue nitro out of those squeegee, Plaza floor, riants asiles, j'y t'eh eeit Tr, Epstein, fil qui, umpiring the hot tub, chockfull of butter, Iota in, out of, the place, their oiled-up, of an Epsilon, minds, herded in skulls, viens vivre, rivers of veins, vero babae babae, not only butter, expired infant formula, dispensationalist body bags, and dour uric acid, every drop, I didn't think much of that bit, but I can't say I loved it. T'eh eeit, t'eh eeit. You know what they say, says the rat. He disgusts me, says the stoned slug, pass the salt. When hee mooueth himselfe, says the cow, he crepeth wyth hys one halfe. I have to say, says the manager. What gets me, says the antelope, is why would God, of all people, do something like that. What could he possibly get out of it that he didn't have already. It's all about him, says the ram. He can't stand it if anyone else gets a look-in. Among all things called one, he has to hold first place. His oneness is not like other onenesses. He is supremely one. Other gods are so fiddly and come in so many bits, only a philistine with its head up its ass would seriously think they were one. It's the kind of controlling behaviour you normally see in domestic abuse, says the pit pony. As has been pointed out on more than one occasion on these very premises, says the manager, they can't say he didn't give them enough notice. I will kill thy root with famine, he said. True, says the tapir, but there are ways of starving everyone to death. Annihilate them and steal all of their land if you have to, but come on, be fair, don't ruin it, you don't have to turn it into an eating contest for American fund managers. They've got enough blood on their hands to last a hundred thousand innocent lifetimes, says the tick, already, it's someone else's turn to eat. He's let himself down, says the lamb, if you ask me. One minute he's all I have heard the groaning of the children, the next thing you know he's chucking boulders out of the sky and splatting them like tomatoes. To shut them up, probably, says the hedgehog, they probably did his head in. He probably just got sick of having to listen to it all day, says the dog, it's worse if you're omniscient, you can't switch off. He should have a word with himself, says the worm, this is strong shit, anyone else feeling it yet. Stop being disingenuous, says the cow. He didn't mean all children. It was perfectly clear what he meant. You know full well it was only the children of Israel that he said he'd bring out from under the burdens. All other Serpents, says the sissy sambar, are horriblie afraide to heare his hyssing, and make a fuss. Waz touc mir ein ze hôhez zil, you say, t'eh eeit, t'eh eeit, says the huss. Where to, says the pig-headed buzzard. Back to front, says the cow, euery one hys way. Look, e, lo, rics, there, in black and white. Enough. Craft and. Ducking. Loosen up, says the eelpout. I stand, I sand me down, I canned the truth. Corrected, I crouch knotted. Hard gates have I gone. Pickle my mother's eyes, says the manager, if it's not time for us to look to our salvations. Our simplicitie, says the. You're shitting me, says the. To be chiselled. There is none. Fümms. Blaw þis trompe. Slug, what already. Of us but hath itching ears, says the goat, when it comes. Like me. To that, devoting their Cities to utter Destruction, as God commanded, there, in black and white, says the pedantic locust, orange and purple and blue. Off. Bö wö. Now in coblas doblas. An escape ramp, basically, for the corner of my eye, where the hindsights and blindspots flock and fly, outlining visions, but the second you spin around, you can't stop, and they're gone, and there you are, spinning around, the second the first second is over, and so on, forever, until the breaking of the day, when all seconds shall be indistinguishable, and there'll be no distinction, and we'll all be white in that heavenly light, because they're all the same second, because you are always spinning around, and it doesn't matter, because it's not really that different from all the other units of time in my life, anyway seconds have only been around for just over a thousand years, what are you drinking, says the pig. My mother's milk, says the cow. Random blood, says the bat. Nothing for me, thanks, says the Palestinian, I'm good. And for you, you say, what exactly can I get you. Light, you hideous group of ills, you say, pints of light. A thousand pints of light, say the ubiquitary consciences, for my comrade here, says the puckish earwig. Will that be everything, says the manager. Got any scratchings, says the pig, I have an extream itch. You're in luck, says the manager. What do you think I will say I want you to give me, says the pig, but will only in the imagination of a pig be what I do actually want. I can't imagine, says the manager. What's left, says the sky. I can't see it. Most things, says the manager, what are you thinking. Don't ask, says the cusk, and you won't receive. Tää zää Uu, pögiff. What the. Eel, says the manager. I had eel, says the pig, already, this day, for my snack. Lead. Not lead. Lead is a bit much. Heater scratchings. Pewit. Teeth. It's too early for teeth, says the pig. Diet. Barn. Don't stop. I'll tell you when you can stop. Mash scratchings. Isosceles scratchings. I do not cherish the illusion that I am a human animal, says the dog, or that I will ever have the patience of a human saint. We non-human animals have our own saints, admittedly, with failings of their own. You don't exactly have to look far. And yet you will not. You ran into one of them in the bathroom, I hear. I'm not saying anything. Our saints may not be like your saints, our saints may eat their own shit, exchange sperm through genital pores in their heads, or spend their entire lives grinding their teeth on the bars of a cage and running on the spot inside a plastic wheel, to give only a few examples, entirely at random, but at least they're not patient. I impose on their heavenly hospitality and call on them to affirm, that I have been waiting to be served, on this day, at this bar, for the past, I don't know, eighty years, and not so much as a wheedling, or mordant, t'eh eeit, t'eh eeit has once escaped my lips, nor did I breathe a word of protest. What do you want, says the manager. And if now, says the dog, you, by the grace of your profession, and aided by the use of one or another of the extremities that you have not yet succeeded in retracting, should be persuaded of the possibility of finding it, somewhere, in the dusty, strip-lit, pissoir of your atrocious heart, sance cracke or flaw, save everywhere, to stop expectorating over your murderabilia for one second, I'd be almost gratifiedly insensible if you'd fetch me up a pint of your undrinkable backwash spiked with Natasha Hausdorff, though if it's all the same to you, as it is to me, I could quite happily terminate in anhydrobiosis, at this hour, all over your sumptuously upholstered recliner, cursing creation, you do know I am not made of yeast. It's fine, take your time. Cork scratchings. Anything but that, says the pig. Lid scratchings. Squeezer scratchings. Botswain scratchings. I'll have a bag of the teeth, I guess, says the pig, if you're telling me that's all you've got.

6

The demand for food is relentless, says the manager, giving everyone hope and a future. We are reaching out, says the dog, regarding recent media coverage, we are shocked and outraged by the actions of two senior regulars, they have been exited. I can hear them chained up outside, says the pig, piteously howling at the unmoved sky. Let them back in, says the plaice, it'll only be someone else. If I can't say what I think, then I don't get to think, says Balaam's ass, and then I'm going to fall into a pit and take everyone else with me. What, says the gritty, disinhibited nit. I think I have made myself clear, says Balaam's ass. No doubt, says the chicken. Run it past me one more time, says the disinhibited nit, humour me. I'm listening this time. I promise. If I can't say what I think, then I don't get to think, and then I'm going to fall into a pit and take everyone else with me, says Balaam's ass. Don't ask me to do it again. That's the last time I'm doing it. What do you mean by saying what you think, says the skink. What do you mean what do I mean, says Balaam's ass. I know what I mean, says the nit, I mean I don't know what you think you mean by think, but it doesn't sound much like thinking to me. I don't think it matters, says the satanic giraffe. You must have something wrong with your ears, says Balaam's ass. I do, says the kangaroo, your mouth. I said it before, says Balaam's ass, and I'll say it again. If I can't say what I think, then I don't get to think, and then I'm going to fall into a pit and take everyone else with me. Always room for one more, says the blob fish. Until there aren't any of them left obviously. Do you want me to give you a moment, says the pig. What else have you got, says the buzzard. Tripe hoops, says the manager. Let me think, says the pig. I'm not a child. Sorry, says the manager. Let me see, says the moose, stop me if I'm way off, you think that if you can't say what you think, then you don't get to think. Is that what you're saying. You heard the man, says the dog. Who are you calling a man, says Balaam's ass. It's a figure of speech, for Christ's sake, says the man, don't shit your jodhpurs, they're crotchless. You know what I mean. Yes, says the pig. All of it. So you only think when you can say what you think, says the mink. I've said everything I am going to say, says Balaam's ass. You did, says the dog. You fucking did it. The thing to remember is, you could easily have fucked it up, but you didn't. What about if your mouth is full of boerewors, or kapok, says the shiftless lark. Or shit, says the pewit. No forced harlequineries, says the manager, read the sign, if it's a cremation furnace you're after. Chuck it all. No, but, seriously, says the barmy winkle, think about it, what if what you say, when you think you're saying what you think, isn't, actually, what you think it is, but is only what you think you want to say you think, so that everyone will think you think it, and you're so excited, and happy, when they do, that you end up thinking you do think it, or at least, so confused, and so delighted, that, in a way, it doesn't matter whether what you think is what you think it is or something you don't think but only think it would be exciting to think. When what really matters, says the mole, is the thing you don't think, the missing thought. And what if you never get to fall into a pit, says the unconvinced anaconda, let alone the sort of pit everyone else is ever likely to want to be taken with you to, when you were the only one who had advance knowledge that anything to do with a pit was even in the offing. What if it's only then, when you're staring down a long future with no pit, that you're able to understand, and think, that all you really wanted all along was to take everyone else with you, when you felt like it, because you were being stopped, somewhere dark and horrible, whether that be a pit or anywhere else, it doesn't matter, provided they didn't want to be there, the variety of hole is not of no little consequence, they can be nowhere if they like. And then by the time you grow up, as an old man, and you worry because you're somehow not as sick of being told off and stopped, and not as titillated by the intellectualization of your strop about being allowed to say what you think as you used to be, in your prime, when you made a success of monetizing your identity, and you think, for the first time, oh no, I'm too late, everyone else is busy, or everyone is off saying what they think they think about something else, in a pit you don't know about, probably, or weren't invited to, that they all got together and dug behind your back, while you were alone, selflessly making love, and when you try, suddenly, in a panic, to round everyone up for your own trip to the pit, all you can manage to scrape together by way of involuntary humanity, when you don't get to say what you think, is a wretched bunch of drifters, a rump, in essence, of the meek, abject vagabonds, who, even if they could by some miracle be multiplied to infinity, would still not even come close to being everyone else, because they're too old, for one thing, and who, under gentle interrogation, are incapable of saying what a pit even is, any more,

and whose leery enthusiasm about being taken
into a pit with you when you fall into one because
you can't say what you think is a real turn-off, not
what you had in mind when you used to fantasise
about taking everyone into pit at all, but you can't
exactly call it off, when they've come all that way,
and anyway, they love you, and you don't want to
have to explain to the few people who could actually
be bothered to show up, on a Monday, in May, that
it's not worth it now, because of who they are, and
suddenly you notice, with horrific relief, that you're
thinking things even you surely don't think, and
then saying them, free as a bird, things like, I think
we've made our point, let's skip the pit, or, maybe we
should wait until more people know about it and are
watching, to maximise the impact, or, nobody said
we have to fall into the first pit we come across, let's
split up and keep looking, or, the thing is, I'm meant
to be at a funeral in ten minutes, or, hang on, I've got
something in my eye.

7

Time for one more, says the manager, you will now proceed to tell me what it will be. You never know, says the carp, your mind might be elsewhere for a reason. Picture it, splashing around in the night sky, flirting with the sacrificed North Koreans, bravely kicking themselves. Slavery is the real international. What isn't, says the dog. I'll tell you, says the llama, my head isn't, why isn't mine working, and where do I go to wait patiently, with my mouth shut, for one that is. My mind's elsewhere, says the flea, too, but it didn't get me anywhere. Depends what you mean, says the anteater, by shut. The mouth can shut in many different ways. That's the beauty of the mouth. Gums first, says the jaguar, or teeth first. Or tongue first. I'm not talking about that, says the toad. Don't waste your breath, says the bucktoothed hen with a broken claw, screw loose, and black eye, you'll be wanting it one day, it'll come in handy when you want to suffocate. Don't leave it too long. Dame handy partridge, ware your pate. There'll be hundreds of thousands of us, soon, says the corpse, you might as well give up. Is that putrescine I can smell, that you're wearing, says the little minx, I like it, it's intolerable, sweet and heavy. If you're not too busy being you, why don't you be too busy being a ruined sky. Hay-scoops, their shadows, says the gaur, addicted to the bodies we were stuck with, given us at random, are leaving them to rot under the rubble of the children's intensive care unit. Now I'll have to speak up, you think. Anyone want to guess where that is. What, says the pretty mahogany bay. What do you mean what, say what you think, you say. Anyone want to guess where what is, says the mahogany bay, you didn't say. O my mind. You've got a funny way of showing it, says the blunt duck. Not now, says the manager, what do you mean. I said my mind is elsewhere, you say, and I invited the room to stay and have a go at guessing where I meant. But answer came there none. Your so-called mind can fuck itself, says the manager. He haþ set is o fot is oþer toforen, says the communist pelican, like a legless centipede. Of course I'm a communist. Bit slow in here tonight, says the sloth. Where is everybody. Good question, says the manager, I'll ask it myself next time I have people round. In a pit, says the pewit, over by the old burning bush. Don't roll your eyes across the floor at me. What do you mean a pit. How many kinds of pit do you think there are. Stop it, screams the pig. I'm trying to think. I'll roll a joint, says the thick-skinned skink. Let's head down there, says the boy, you owe me, anyway they'll never let you in. What about me, says the dog, do they let dogs in, I'll let them have a suck on this. Con dulces estruendos de bélicas salvas, says the pig, you're laughing, whistling there's a place for us out of a fluted tear duct. Do you know what, says the divinatory chicken, you're letting yourself in for. No, you say, do I want to know. No, says the negative chicken. No dogs, says the manager. Get that dog out of here. No, you say. I've got to draw the line somewhere. Leave him alone. The sheep shall be eaten by the wolf, says the manager, it's human nature. Leave some for us, says the lamb, you pig, whatever, I don't care. If the sheep don't get eaten by the wolf, what's the point in being the wolf. I'd still rather be the sheep, says the wolf. I'd love it if one day, when I was nibbling the turf, I ate me, for it was fate. Where is everybody. It's dead in here tonight. Can I come in, says the boy. You'll have to leave first, says the she-frog. Will you go with me, says the boy. Do I look like your mother, says the sky. Don't let me leave, they won't let me back in. Why would anyone want to come back in, though, really. Look around. What, I like it here. I don't get any grief for being me, or half. Everyone leaves me alone. I'm sorry, says the she-frog, I don't understand, can you speak a lot more slowly. Can you speak very, very slowly, and can you use different words, you keep cutting out, like a tongue. I can't, you say. Can't what. Speak, you say. I can't, I don't know the words. What's it like, is it a relief. What I'll say is, you don't know what you're letting pain in for, you say. Says the gaur. But you can't exactly leave your heart waiting outside, in oiled-up snow, behind the world. You'll soon warm up once you're in, says the cow. Time for bed, says the manager, now please, and, O, die Lust steigt schön allmählich mit der Rechnung. Steep my galls in honey, compañeros, the goats are the price of the field, give me all your money, says the pig. I'll get these, says the dog. You can't take it with you. Not you as well, says the skate, I have enough on my plate, as the psychopathic reservists step, geese-like, over his skinny corpse, says the kangaroo, into the nightmare of really existing Jerusalem.

8

Get that down you, says the dace, for every drop of that ought to be down you. Come back when that is down you, and we'll see. See what, says the dog. Wait and see, says the mayfly, I won't keep you. Come back, says the po-faced pig. Money, says the vampire bat, is evil, might as well use it while you've got it. I can't, says the furniture beetle, I'm too unhappy. What does everyone want. What is everyone going to have. Stondet all stille, says the pig, stille, stille, stille, chartreusish and papery, stille as any ston, like an embroidery hoop, and looked back at me and said, it's you, I can't believe it. Trippe a lutel wit thi fot. The whole night I'd been in pieces, gesturing on the sly toward a pitcher of contaminated rainwater at the far end of the bar for show. I can't reach, I'd say, throwing my voice, not giving a fuck where it lands as long as it didn't flatten anybody. Spend and God shall send, says the manager. Spare and ermor care. The bar top, says the pig, that not five minutes ago was buffed to such a shine you could shimmy the length of it on your knees without taking the majority of your skin off, now is yet again covered with barbed wire and lard. Pop your heart back in and I'll give you a shove, you'll be upset in no time, says the dog. I'm quite capable of giving myself a shove myself, says the limpet. What else have you got, says the goat. If you've even got anything. Speak for yourself, says Balaam's ass. Hello, says the Englishman, emboldening those who seek to dismantle accountability. The Englishman is sick of always having to be the straight man, while the Irishman always gets to be the one who says the funny shit that comes third. Try being me, says the Palestinian newborn, you wouldn't last five minutes. The problem with reality, says the Muscovy duck of the Rio Grande Valley, is it's inefficient. You have to take the threaded arm bit that's attached to the circularity frame, shorten it, maybe take the pin, or bolt, out of the top bracket, bend that bracket to make the arm fit tighter and stop it all sagging, or the hinges get loose on the door and it makes the closer jump like mad. Not bad, says the sad, stupid langoustine. I like a nice vanilla reality. I will never believe that, says the cormorant. Are you blind, says the mink. Anyway, everything gives up after holding out. Love, democracy, peace, life, justice, childhood, happiness. No point, says the saucy beaver, being all humane about it. Fördert unsrer Sprachenschmuk, says the skunk. Exactly, says the. We'll have a little less, says the manager, of that, if you don't mind, there's children present. And women, says the hippo. And men, says the pig. And a big hole in the ground, says the sky. What are they doing here, says the raccoon. Tell me something, says the Englishman. Ok, says Balaam's ass, there's no easy way to say this, sit down, you were adopted. Where's the toilet, says the camel, I'm about to piss all over the coffins. Right, you louts, says the manager, out with your genitals. Line up. All the way down, please. There, says the Englishman. I am already in line. What do you mean, says the manager. There, says the Englishman. There what, says the manager. That, says the Englishman. That what, says the manager. What, says the Englishman. That, says the manager. What, that, says the Englishman. Yeah, says the manager, that, what do you think I'm pointing at. That's the window, says the Englishman. My turn, says the koala, voilà. What do you think you're you doing, says the manager. What, says the window. That, says the manager. What, that, says the camel. Yeah, says the manager, that. That's the window, says the koala. I thought that was the window, says the manager. Who told you that, says the dog. He did, says the manager. He literally just said it. Hands up who still has hands, says the detainee whose hands had to be amputated, says the dog. That's because of the shackles they use on all the unanaesthetised civilians they shot at the field hospital in the Negev desert, says the preppy bonobo. If everybody talks, says the manager, at once. My turn, says the man. No need, says the manager, put it away. My turn, says the legless salmonid. Why don't you take a photo. My god, says the manager, what's that. What, says the salmonid. That, says the manager. What, that, says the Englishman. Yeah, says the manager, that, stop fucking me. That's. Around. The sky, says the ostrich, where's the catch. I don't believe it, says the manager, I can't believe this is happening, there's no catch. My turn, says the bobby calf, keep your eyes peeled. Make it snappy, says the manager, we've all got somewhere we'd rather be. Of the pig. You call that having somewhere. Satisfied, says the dog. Says. The bee. No, says the window, I'm faking it. My god, says the manager, what's that. Says the burbot, as a hobby. What, says the dog. That, says the manager. That, says the floor. Yeah, says the manager, what do you think I'm talking about, that. That's a load of dead bodies, what do you think it is, says the hippo, a sausage roll, where do you want it. Everywhere, says the furniture beetle. This, says the camel, is getting ridiculous, I have to go somewhere. Yet here you still are, says the manager, and here I still am, undeterred, over-budget, light years from the crossing in the dark. I'll take your word for it, says the camel. It's not mine, you say, but you're welcome. What, only one. There, says the sloth. And though we two may be separated by an abyss, impassable as is the little grave whose gap uncrossed keeps earth and heaven apart, to stop them glassing each other, I'll never give up regretting I didn't have your relatives evacuated. What do you call a sty, says the deer, with no way in or out. You need your heads examining, the pair of you, says the burbot, I'm speechless. That, says the dog. You've lost me, says the manager. If only, says the clam, if only I had lost you. You'd know where to look, says the manager. Thank god for the walls. I'd rather drink my own neurotoxic saliva spiked with crop milk through a straw made of hundreds of LSD tabs, says the solenodon, making a face, than another mouthful of this Argentinian muck. Nobody is suggesting we do nothing, says the cat. All taken care of, says the lamb. I have a frisky little beaujolais, if you're not particular, says the manager. Aren't we doing that already, though, just by being alive, says the squid. I get it. It has to stop. We can't, says the dottyback, just stand here and let it happen. Is that thing with you, says the manager, it's not dead is it. It's not dead, says the dog, it's just had a long day. It's my heart.

9

See you later, life, then, you said, I'll be off now then. Ok, bye, I'm off. I didn't make myself clear. What life did you expect, though. Nou hit is ant nou hit rys, insinuation's nth youth. Qualis nox, shut up, I'm trying to think, fuit illa, shady as hell, but real as well, says the skint skink, you know. Where do we think we even are going, dressed like this. Watch out for flying aid pallets, says the duck. You don't want to be killed. Or decapitated, says the chicken. Trust me, fuck that. Beyond words, says the hyena, there is a bit of peace and quiet. It's in our DNA, says the legless centipede. Get your feet, says the abyss, off my boring flooring. Ignore him, says. Poor you. Souls. Off. The pig. Are igneous, no, says. Hip bone. Scant. Ignipuncture. The skink. I am organic. Neck it, says the spiny sea. Dressed like crab. Skinny. Gone. Cucumber. Says. Tomba ignuda. Th'ulcerous, gowtie. It. Off, says. Says here, says. Connected. Ignore them. The dandiacal candiru, that the slighted H. Sorry. NWIS are off. Oh no, says the dwarf pygmy goby, why. Duck, says the duck. They are a vital source of forex revenue, says the pit pony. That was close. What's that, says the kangaroo rat. The corpses or this thing, says the candiru. That thing, says the kangaroo rat. This, my wroth friend, is the new Henley and Partners Wealth Migration Report, says the candiru. I didn't get to the end, says the gerenuk. But we're all one. Spring soon, says the dog. Beasts of burden, says the lamprey, smell the barley of Kedropolis. Airdrop me a medium. Pig. Sunk in blind. Sink. Ignavia. In the igneduct. In. Or swim. Easy. In. Igne incidit. For you. Ate. Et. Help me. To say, says. Crebritate. Albeit. Arbeit. Igne expiari. Next, says. Flat lewdnesse and bouerie, says the cow, I'm not particular. Ignore her, says the. Demergitur. Doe. O God. Because you have a mouth. Shewing great tokens. And. Let's go and die all over his golf course, says the swan, there's always one. You know. Fire away. The ant. By fire diddest. Delivery for the yak. Get. How. On with it. Me. To use it, albeit not really, says. Says the yak, what is it. It's. They're. Says. Am I. Looks like. Sufferedst the bush. We. Getting on a. Waiting by. The hen. Alone. The tanks. Burgers. To burn. There is no nation that feeds its. Bit. And. And yet not. I like it, says the goat. O God. Floorless. Up for it. Foorthwith. To consume. Let. Fries. Him that. The floor-length ray. I. And onion. Duck, says the. Is. Accused. Chicken. Yes, says the duck. No, I. Beare it. Mean duck. Sealed. Good dog. Says the dog, vp for. Says. Moo. Into the darkness is not necessarily forward. Oh no. The space of three. I'm famished. Upon our minds. The duck. Quack. Rings. Daies. What's got. What's got. If burns, guilty. Four wheels. I did. Crack open a chicken. And flies. Into him, says. Day after. Don't. Wing. Day. Window. Know, says the swallow. The capybara. Kwashiorkor. Why. What. People will use different words. Is he not. From what. A garbage truck, says the fly. Moving. I would. That pallet he's under might. The distance into which the future is vanishing, says the skate, seriously, look at the state of it. Have some flour. Questa la sorte, says the drooling otter, delle umane genti, very droll. Life. Left in it. Ordalian. On behalf of a mind. On its knees, out of a dog bowl. Abide tribulation. To hell with degrees. What a night that was, on that soft-looking bed, encircled by sound, says the sky. Nec curo, say the painted butterflies, a storm is near, where's the crevice. Seek, says the deer. One swig, says the nit, of your full cup, or snifter, nobody arrives in an instant to the extremity of malice. That said, says the orca, with respect, who needs anything going on in there to be able to be assumed to be syntactically definable, when you can make do with a chew toy and some axiomatic constraints. Or just shoot everything that moves, says the possum. Fuck me, says the nit, one shiver of a lousy drip. I'm not a micromanager, says the manager.

10

What do you call a pack of orcas that shorts the MSCI ETF days before the Hamas attacks. A thousand years are but as one day, in my opinion. I'm quietly confident about my mind. That policy expired ages ago, says the nurse shark. In the golden age of depleted uranium. Long, long shift. Short shrift, says the peafowl, wiþoute fyne. Unaccountable, says the unau. It blows my mind. And swallows. On account of the projected saving in psychic energy, otherwise destined to be frittered on repression, I'm afraid, says the pig, embarrassingly, it must be said, considering the nugatory value of the marginal propensity to save. To say nothing, says the dog, interesting. Eternal inflation, says the sarcastic arctic tern, and its macabre Rafahi reducibility candidates, are always on my mind. I, says the nurse shark, expect direction from our common head. I make bold. It's neck and neck, says the aardvark, with meaning. Until you come barging in. Sleep, says the pepperweed. Tell it to a fuller breast, says the moose, loosen up, desire the sincere milk of the word. Words, says the lion, are for vermin, don't begrudge them, the little angels, they've had a rough time of it. Time, says the barracuda, is either long or short, you can't have it both ways. Don't talk to me about feet, says the alligator. I just walked miles, as fast as my legs will carry me, across scorching sand, chewing my way through wire fencing, terrified I'd be shot, drones constantly buzzing overhead, dehydrated and forsaken, to petition a heavily armed psychopath for a serving of lentils, after I escaped from the concentration camp in DeSantis country, next to Parviz Sabeti's Apollo chair. The place of the feet is the disposing of them in their proper rooms, says the plaice. That's not a million miles away from what I mean, says the manager, when I say many other things. My own business, when. Before. After. What were they thinking, says the lamb, that they'd all just walk away, and no-one would get murdered. Humanity doesn't grow on trees, it's nailed on. Somebody ought to tell them. Kingyo no fun, says the knackered kangaroo, quod oculis, þe dede wyþ-oute, þe grantinge wyþinne, dum video, gilts, bongs, gongs, the gulf impassable of Sleep, fluid retention, hell on earth, you know, general knowledge. Can you be a bit more completely atonal, says the kinorhynchan, all this morbid finicking with pseudodisharmonic modulations makes it hard to keep caring about the thing we're here to do. Wipe that smirk off your face, says the nit, with a damp petal, gently, up and down, now in slow, teasing, circles. The wil is heet, I ween, says the hyena, but the subpoena is hoot. I rejoice in a thing of nought, says the huss. That's taking things a bit far, says the chicken, even Trump, de luy parlar me duelh, likes his buds with a touch of the old pouting ripeness that tempts the taste, that's Farquhar, and he's our apex predator. Ask me anything, says the sky, and may the coming world arrive to you full fraught with all your wishes. If nobody else has got one, says the sea cow, I'd quite like to hear the one about the Swiss affiliate and the Moscow branch of the Armenian National Interests Fund, yet again, and I'd like you not to leave out the outmoded bit about the CAT scan slice of the propugnacles of David Papazian's battered abdomen after that legendary night out on the psychoactive contrast agents. What a horror show that was, pizdets. Not that again, says the manager, who knew. Nature calls, says the dog, you a cunt. Not these tones, says the turkey, these tones. When you've got to go, you've got to go, says the doe, when you've got a minute. The Swiss affiliate is for donors who may prefer to participate outside of the US structure, says the dog. Can we not, says the pig. Off with his snout, says the nit, I am totally drunk, but only a bit merry. Let him finish, says the gaur, and let me finish. Let us be done with it, as it is done with us. Three hundred or so US contractors, says the boa constrictor, feathering their nests, bristling with flails, arbalests, chakrams, bastons à feu, language and rhetoric, sulphur, cream pies, and scythes, say to the excited crowd, who could eat a horse, come and get it, says the dog. Don't, says the pig. What's on the menu today, says the crowd. God, says God, every time I come in here. Patience, says the nit. Give it a second. You'll like this. Anthropomorphs, Detroit City Shield goons, stuffed to the eyes with University of Michigan doubloons, says the duck, blaze like meteors. What I'm hearing is, ethical philosophy reënters the arena, says the cormorant, and everyone is like, oh shit. Make way, says the duck, we are all coming through. Good dog cannot be too tart in his jests, says the pig, if he doesn't want a trotter up the muzzle. You, says the dog, will die in terror in an industrial slaughterhouse, stuck through the chest, your brachiocephalic trunk severed, to make you bleed out, whereas I will die being stroked in my basket, next to the radiator, by crying children. Fair enough, says the pig. But the US contractors want it to be a surprise, so they tell the crowd they have to come and look in the box, says the dog. The box has a black sticker on the side with a white logo on it that looks like a kind of modernist dove, right next to the infamous initialism. If anyone else is bored out of their skull, or anyone else's, says the pig, I'm off to the little boy's room for a line of shit. How outré you are, says the centipede, I'd join you but I'm off to the little piglet's room for a fisting, a trottering, a beaking, a proboscising, and a winging, at the end of which we all hold each other and cry. I'm torn, says the tick, furtively having its DNA tested in the basement of the Turgenev Museum at the Ratmir-ADS Christmas party you crashed, says the sozzled dog, over a cracked goblet of GosNIIOKhT crop agents, while the Delaware outfit kept its proverbial back turned doing head-stands on baby field mice and the families they can't feed and in fairness shouldn't have been allowed to have. What do lawyers wear to court, says the ewe. Are you going to tell us what happens next, says the crane, did they look in the box or not. As if the future had nothing better to do than hang around waiting for us. I'm way ahead of you, says the dog. He's behind you, says the chicken. I'm right behind you, says the dog. Don't leave me hanging. Lawsuits, says the ewe. Pound, says the kangaroo, said keep it for the men who insist on knowing. The thing is, most of them turned out to be assholes, at bottom. I get hard just not thinking about it. Do you know what, says the dog, I've had enough. Of, says the pig. Look who's back, says the manager. Run out of nares, did we. Don't leave me holding the bag, says the kinorhynchan, I don't want to get caught. Je est, says the batty kangaroo, un autre jeu du poète quand il s'arme de l'action dramatique. Don't rub it in, says the rat, I'm still sore. I mean, not unless you're positive you're comfortable. You've lost me, says the manager. I wish. What's red and bad for your teeth, says the tick, a brick. Slow down, says the camel, I'm thick but I would like to get it too. Where are you going with this. I flatter myself I'm not going anywhere, says the dog. Not without you, comrade. We will not be moved, says the fly. Anyway we've got all the long night long. Don't mind him, he's, says the sand crab. We all know what you mean, says the walrus, you can stop tapping that claw on the blow-hole in your forehead, do you mind if I stick a straw in that. Alright, says the dog, I'm only doing this once. Everyone shut up. So, it's winter. I'm writing a book of jokes. The jokes are funny, everyone loves them. Yeah right. I'm thinking maybe I'll pitch it to RCW literary agents. Yeah like they'll want you. Then one day, I'm doing some research, just dicking around on the internet really, for this joke I'm working on about the hundreds of starving children murdered by the GHF, you know, it's interesting what you find when you poke around a bit under the covers. Felix qui diligitur. You're telling me, says the alligator. So the GHF is headquartered in Delaware, but they set up a quoteunquote affiliate branch in Geneva, for investors who prefer to operate outside US structures. Nothing to see there. One of the three dickheads who run GHF is an Armenian reportedly living in the UK. Let's go and burn his house down, says the dove, in our dreams, like fractal suet. He used to be at the Armenian National Interest Fund, until one day his contract was prematurely terminated pending a little hiccup involving the unexplained transfer of millions of dollars from the ANIF to its Moscow branch. Everyone loves a taste of scandal, says the kākāpō. Probity is to plutocracy as puberty is to polyamorous perversity, says the pygmy tyrant.

No kinkshaming, says the manager, will ever be despotic enough. So you see where this is headed, says the dog, I omit, as a matter impertinent. Disgusting, says the lamb. Where do you find this stuff. That's a matter of opinion, says the ibis. Knock knock, says the tortoise, and it shall be opened. All that loot pumped out of the Armenian proletariat, says the gaur, and for what. It didn't happen in a vacuum, says the cow. Hurry up, says the pig, we'll be here for eternity at this rate. Sorry, says the dog, anyway, this same Armenian got the nod from Trump to head up the relief effort in Gaza, says the dog. Is that it, says the pig. The GHF has lots of American investors who shall remain nameless, says the stork. Like us, says the teary halibut. The Israeli state has shovelled hundreds of millions of shekels into the GHF in secret, down the laundry shaft into the offshore accounts of you know who, while Netanyahu's ministers deny, hand on heart, that down is down. Humanity doesn't come cheap, says the chicken. It'll blow over, says the whelk. Give it a lot more time. Stay strong. Well done, says the manager, now you've gone and masturbated my one regular. I'll be back, says the olm, just crawling out for a quick look at the screaming sky. Don't stare, says the raven. It hates it. Don't wait for me, you can always repeat the entire thing from the beginning. Hurry up, says the bos mutus, I'm gasping. 1100 per day plus a 10000 signing bonus, says the dog, who wouldn't sniff at that. Unless. Peanuts, says the chimpanzee, to the suits who get to polish off the carnage, and not even a whiff of chickenfeed to their masters, but serious money to a working man with mouths to feed and children of his own to keep alive.

11

You know, it's funny, my wife asked me this question a few days back, says the giant penguin. What did you say, says the chicken. What was I supposed to say, says the giant penguin, I tried to get it into her head that it's all ancient history and it's no use her getting all cavernous and extinct but she had to go and. Don't tell me, says the mesel. Even the jugs, says the badger, horrendously. Pots, says the pig. What, says the lamb. Pots, says the pig. Pots, not jugs. Two pots. If you'll let me finish, says the giant penguin. Not saucepans, says the ceiling mirror. And she wasn't having it, she kept on at me. You wish, says the lamb. Till I broke down and told her everything, says the giant penguin, was lost. We're never going to get out of here, says the lamenting mother, I hedde a sone nou haue I non I not in world whoder to gon. I told her to drop it, but she wouldn't let it go. What was in the jugs, says the badger. If you're going to be stupid, says the manager, it's ok, I'm here, don't be scared. One in eight of the prescribed drugs available through the NHS, says the trade minister, as I understand it, says the burbot. Pots, says the pig. Yeah, says the giant penguin, no shit, two pots, duo altissima dolia bullientia, one for boiling water, one for whipped cream, red garra, and Himalayan salts infused with bergamot. Time drives everything before it, says the owl. Where is everybody, says the egg, I am so alone. What did she say to that, says the chicken. The usual, says the manager. Amend. She said, so, you actually saw it did you, you went up and looked in them, says the giant penguin, and I. It's okay, I only have super fish oil injuries, says the mesel. Help, says the. Eny oþur doublehed, says. I've done that, says. It was great, you can really feel them snacking on your corns. Told you, I said, there was a kind of shining thread, I had it wound round my, wait, it led. Let her speak, says the. Me wonteþ boþe weole and wit, says the. Me there, I followed it. You proceeded thither, says the pig. Don't tell. When, guided. Therein, up to. To gratify, says. Fear not, Lord. His spleen. Not me. Me. Thighs. Assisting my eyes, personalised. Soþ. Neon LED, one for antimony pentafluoride, bits of hair, and TEVA shares, one for coconut milk. Stop that blood-curdling wailing, says the manager. All whom you have beheld. She didn't know. I told her to close the door on the way back in, say. Trembling. One for anti-theft spikes, crap poetry, and Canaan, one for the breast, Cuyp's sunsets, and enough time. I don't believe it, she said, says. Undergo. The giant penguin, rolling. Jugs is funnier, says the dog, I can't get out. To drop it. These torments, designated. Next I pass. She's sangria than ever. To reset the dial around commercial relationships, says the. One for all for Azazel, virulent action potentials, cheap and nasty life, America, and swill, one for dreams of flying, humanity, the sun, and lobster. Adoun I. Like Niobe, says the dog. Let me explain. Bear with me, says the lamb. Have the decency, says the. The proximal. Manager. End of the bone, two articular facets, one for. This lip-wise age, says, suddenly, an oval, shallow concavity, looking. Don't. Upwards and a little. Start, says. The badger. The giant penguin. Inwards, one. Put a sock in. Do they enjoy it, says the sky. It, I. Other, external, quadrilateral, slightly convex. Told her, says the. From before backwards, slightly concave. Giant penguin. One for shrapnel, Dr Phil, no bliss save that of rapid gain, clapped out Tavors, teeth sunk in an arm, skid marks, pitch, Thiers, the bad object, canned laughter, and mass starvation, one for state ownership, ears, ample methylphenidate, stair lifts, relaxing with friends, chromatic polyphony, Wieners's lust, health, the 1947 revolt of the Kikuyu women, water, and nice skin. One for cheese-paring and oblivion, one for sativa and dactyls. One for greuoushed's stings, one for wyldehed's tongs. One more, says the perky cockle. Non è più tempo di parole, says the manager. I can give you a plastic. You had to knock the evil out of a person, says. It's. Please. Our royal race. This is a. Barings. Wondrous witty age that sees beyond the truth of things, forty degrees, says the dog, at last. Or fifty, says the pig. Or fifty. At last. Repent. I bet she wanted to know how to get out, says the strange bird, of one and into the other. Absolutely, says the giant penguin. You're fading, says the chicken, you're breaking up. Don't we all, says the pig. Don't be pre-historic, says the chicken. Will you help her out, says the lamb, if it comes to that. I wonder what she's up to now. I wonder, says the pig.

12

Obnazhenie, says the dog, down the hatch. Fetch, says. Not the hatch, says. The baboon, tossing. The scarab, I don't. Because he wanted to make a clean getaway, like the trace of the fugitive gods, tomorrow belongs to the bin. Like them. Sing us. Som in fayth lepe over the hache, they had no tyme to seche the lache, says the senile lark, get. One of your zaghareet, and. Your foot off my. Sutche haue the kirnells eaten all, says the diabolical bobtail squid. You, elephant shrew, says. That gnawes the harts of men. The herd. Such as, says. No clapping, remember. Of wildebeest. Giblets, says the cranky slug. I beg. Someone's been rioting in the abundance of his animal indulgencies, says the manager, the moment my back was turned. I've had enough of tomorrow, says the fly. It's a figure of speech, says the dog. Why speech, says the scarab. Moules, screams the manager. Somebody please tell me somebody here ordered the moules. You have it, says God. It's all yours. Labour to get much of it in your vessels. Speak for yourself, says the lippy platypus. Did you hear the one about the jellyfish with severe acute malnutrition from the Jabalia camp who loved making portable cases for arrows, says. Between you. The posh hippo. Your pardon. What do you mean arrows, says the Irish. And me, says the fried. Man. Don't. Did we. Tell me nobody. Egg. Order the. Ordered the. Moules. Moules. Says. Says. The yolk sac. The manager, I must be losing my mind. Or worse, finding it, says the pig. What, says the. Or finding it, I said, says the pig. Like archery arrows, do you. Finding what, says the. Mean. Mind out, says the manager, it's hot. Never. Hake. Hake. I'd. Mind, says the pig. No go on. For that which befalleth the sons of men befalleth beasts, even one thing befalleth them, as the one dieth, so dieth the other, says. Hearing one day that. Yeah, we all have one breath, says the dog. The baboon. Says the sky, I'm listening. Excuse me, says the desert toad, I was trying to have my say. Sorry, says. As I was about to say, hearing one day that my good friend the. Do they do food, says the. Coffin with stickers of that pyramid from the Cleveland Industrial Worker, glitter, and bits of hair all over it, says. Flywheel. My dreams are a nightmare. The hake. Hearing one day that my good friend the mother was under. Pastor Moore, says the ant. Just moules, says the Scotsman. Says the Irishman. Let him speak, says the pig, or we'll be here all night, all tomorrow night, and all tomorrow night, and all tomorrow night. I'm glad somebody is listening, says the. Like to have a neck that's upside-down. Desert. It was a huge missed steak, says the lamb. Toad. Says. Start again from the beginning, if you like, says the pig. I will, says the desert. Hearing one day that my good friend the mother was under. Anyway, says the pig, he's not the only one with a pair of vestigial claws round here, don't believe everything you hear from Answers in Genesis. The giraffe. Toad. My dear mother, I said, blushing, a surgeon, chase him away, I'll mix you a draught more appropriate to your constitution, in the mean time, drink this. I soon returned. You have a way, says the hen, with words. I have, says the pig, my reasons. I soon returned with my potion, if you don't mind, but the frightening deformity of the pendulous. Moules, screamed. Lip still. The mammal in question, meanwhile, brooded on the vast abyss, did it, says, blood everywhere, scrubbing itself off, says. I'd like to have a floor like that, says the vice president. The newt. Of JDA Worldwide, says the newt. Remained. The manager. It was Madame de Staël, unless I'm psychotic, says the hippo. I said obnazhenie, says the dog. I'll hear you the next time, says the pig. Who called that the thinking part of mankind, or am I thinking of something else. Not entirely, says the pig. I'd like to have been brutally murdered. Did you hear about the sale they're having at the paddle shop, says the boar, it was quite the oar deal. Too, says the speckled. How are we today in there, says the smiling eel, ruffling my hair and knocking on the top of my head, like a door, says the bat, with no mat. Front or back, says the. Revolving. Flywheel. The hake. What do you call a dog magician, says the baboon, a Labra. In diesem Einen Organismus des Rechts, auch ent. Eel. How do I feel, says. I'll have them if they're going, says. Halten ist das Rechts. For real, says. I'm starving, says the. Heel, says. Cadabrador Retriever. Did you hear Satan is going bald, says the hip. Don't. Po, yeah, there's gonna be hell toupee. Leben der Einen unendlichen. Talk shit. Menschheit, says. It, says. The stickleback to. The free, for free. The hippo. The bat to. Slug. Child to. The dog to. The pop-up. The baited hook. I'm not running, says the manager. The sky. Its screaming mother. Itself, under the mirror. Notification. A charity here. I don't. Look out of that window I just smashed, says the chicken, tell me what you'll never see. L'hanno in custodia i Saggi, says the pig. Get it. Blunt foiles were on sharpe pointed Rapiers set, something like that, says the yolk. I don't do it on porpoise, says. Sac. The future. Says the. I love it in here, says the snake. I don't care. Egg. You know

where you are, says the manager, with seafood. What
am I, chopped liver, says God. I'll have to eat them
myself.

13

Can I get the check, please, says the salp. Thus far he.
Carcass. If you think for one minute, says the mole,
rhinestone immunoglobin. Cielos, look what the cat
dragged in. I'm going to stand here. Says. And listen.
Says. Odin. Nod off. The skinny cat. You droning
on. Thus much. You're in luck, says the manager. All
night about the frog in your stomach. And more
by. I've got one. Hearsay. Stachelschwein burger left.
I knew it. Celui qui croit avoir une grenouille dans
l'estomac, though. Back. Else. When. You're out.
You. What more. Wish. Of. I'm thinking. Thought
thought. Can I. We. Be. Do. Your mind. Says. Was.
Would come. For you. To this. I think you need your
ears, says the jerboa, examining. Free. Quiet, I'm
trying. Of having the full English. ɪᴄᴄ. The eastern
tube-nosed. Back. Bat, everyone. To be snails, says
the snail. Is sick of. When you thought. To have
my songs ripped off by that Kochav while. Knows
what. The luminous. You're. Detail. Trying. Is of
no avail. To do. Round here, you pert. Begging for.
Little human. Flour. Shield. You smell like a pencil
sharpener, says the earwig. Speak for yourself, says
the self. I can't stay long, says the. It's. Made Gaur,
the. Shut that baby up, says the manager, I can't
hear. Kind of. Kids. Yeah I remember. Myself think.
That, says. You're missing the point, says the dog.
Anyone know if the. Says who, says. You. The peg, so
much was lost. The peg. Pig's coming tonight, says.
Count me. Forever. I'm going. And many things

have changed their shape and form, and. To say. To kill that. That. The Stachelschwein burger is. Says. One of those things. Out. What soldier of the good old days doesn't fondly remember the three-tiered battalion square. Die linken Beine flogen in die Höh. Hen one. Don't. Day. Mind. The hen. Him. The dog. Says the batty kangaroo, he's had one. Says the kip. L'inanité de ce qui est, Nobel prizes all round, ceux qui succombent méritent de succ. English, says the Huanren. Omber. Per. Frog. Parce qu'ils ont des armes. What did the superannuated child veterans of the CIA snowfall ops. Same again, says the aardvark. Moins. Human. Same again, says the aardvark. Tossed some change to blow up schools and bury people alive say. Relations man. Same again, says the aardvark. At the trusted provider of operational and security. Puissantes. Support services, says. Anyone. Leur. The go-to alias. Don't. Know. Know, says. If. The stork, what. The pig. Did. Is. They say. Infériorité. Don't tell me, says the. Keep it down, says the sea otter. This is a family. Stachelschwein. Yes we can. Burger. How many. Too many. Establishment. Mexicans. No I'm fine, says the. Advise on best. Peg. Practices for engaging with affected. Leere und Mono. Populations, local authorities, and community-based organizations and facilitate dialogue and trust-building, give us a. I don't like to eat on an empty stomach, says the dog. Got anything. To. Humanitarian Liaison Officer. Does it take. Nie. Raving homeless people frequently accost us on the street and with his sweet flesh cram each hollow gut. So how. A bit. Change. Stronger. About it. But semantic surprise. Coming. I was like. From night's dull prison comes the duck, says the brainsick snipe. Tonight. The nation's soul. My head. Explique. Is killing me. Affects the brain.

And she was like. Says. Nice souls, mummy's got
a. The humphead. Differently from. Treat for you.
Just. Wrasse, says. Ifie et. Other surprises. Légitime
le. Like. Well look who decided to grace us, says
the frog, with, we've been. Say when, says the
manager. Syntax. Wondering. When, says the dog.
Your stomach appears. All night when you were
going. Ur écrasement. To be. To show. Talking, says
the rolling. Up. Pin, to the. No. What can I get. Pig.
You. Nothing, says the pig. I can't. Care can. Open
your feet, says the duck. What. Sorry, I mean. Says.
Pass thy gate. Open. Stick around. And passioning.
Did you hear about the restaurant in the casino.
Not art. That feeds its cows. Your eyes. Still. Feet
is funnier. Compassionate. You're killing me. Yeah,
some gamblers prefer high steaks. Says the skinny.
Says the. Spit. Cat. Dog. It. Say. Out, says. Says the
flour. It like. The. You mean it. Behung with crape.
Ayahuasca. Haddock. Give me strength, says the
manager.

14

Egg sounds. Who's there. Eggs. Oh eggs, good. No. Good. No eggs. No good. Eggs sounds good. Not there. Eggs. No, I'm good. You want some eggs. No, I'm good. Oh but you like eggs. Doesn't eggs sound good. No it doesn't. Eggs doesn't sound good, to me. Eggs sounds very bad. Eggs sounds angry. No eggs not angry eggs happy. Eggs like going in head. Not all the way in. Yes eggs go all the way in, they love it there. I am not there. I. I egg on. Entwickelt das E. I am not there. I. Eier der Eulen. Egg phone. Eggs remain in a pile. A' feljül úszó hibás tojások, one little spoon. One spike. One way out of this. There is nothing but a beast, above a beast. There is, says one, nothing above us. Just more beast. More me, says the other, for the rest of us. Don't be stupid, says the daft emu, don't. There's genocide and there's genocide. One little spoon. Be like that. They thought they all mattered the same. But nobody can really love everyone. I loved a few of them, as well as I knew how. Most of them I couldn't love, because they weren't mine. I was never going to let them get away with that. I told the ones that were mine to get rid of the rest. I had a big clean out. Their parents will not see them grow up. They will see them in a heap of carnage, so unimaginably hideous, the trauma will be worse than any pain any of you will ever experience, I told mine. Because I love you. It's not easy being me. People are so ungrateful. They have no idea. A' feljül úszó hibás tojások, one throne.

Phone for egg. Addled and lost. Nervous Liquor. Egg coat. Eggs, says the pig. What prate ye praty pyggysny, says the imperial snipe. Eggs, says the pig, you little shit. Pass the dregs of wit, says the daddy wren, I'm too parched. The aforesaid, the heirs, the said. The manager, in here. Thoroughbred. To the tenements aforesaid. Crispin Odey's head. What's that smell, says the. As set. You look run. Manager. Just. The company a-gaping. Think. Down, says. What. The dog, do. It will. You might need a hand. Mean. Nothing, says. Eggs. With that. To. The cagey bee, mind. Future. I'll manage, says the manager. Your own. The. And this he is ready to aver. Yes, says the manager. Is he, says the pig, is he. Or pleasure. Business, as. Just as we. Paul said. Whereas. I thought. Eggs. Don't. I think it. Even think. Says the skink, I think it was. About. Lid. Per. Looks nice. Eggs glassing. On. Up. Eggs. It's a lot. Chaunc't maynot. The pig in here. Be that. You, it. Up. I just. Sem. Bad-hoovered. Blent. And the sabzevar. Tombant. Says the manager, sur la terre. Away. Go. Go away. No. I was just. I'd like to have a crack at being sane, says the aardvark. Eggset, says the sky. Vouloir s'ouvrir. I hear you. They're your ears. What. Says the. You're saying. Fund. Eggs. I can't believe you said that. Well I can't believe you said that. Eggs. Says the manager. Manager. Your wife. Is it. Doubtless it. Les Enfers. And kids. Open mic night. Were finer. Tonight, says the. Stick. Could we go along. I know a wife. Your name. Always in the way. One, says. Eggs. Of music. In the hat. The trolleyed sky. Besides. If you have one, that. The muskrat. Just. Is. Who doesn't, says. Eggs. It's less. The basketed earth. Hassle if you just stick. One more, then. I don't. A shit ton. I'm gone, says the dog. Says the dog, answer to. I, dog, swear. Eggs. I go. Of frogs in his bed and kneadingtrough.

I take it. By the name. Anything. Dog. Egg. It you. The octopus. Would like to sing. Pigs hate that. Says us something. Odeyhead. Learn how to speak. Egg. The gaur. First. I'm not deaf, says the pig. Up tonight we. I've never met herbivore. Have the. Have the. Et. Have the. Have the spotted crake. Locusts said. Suet. They'll do. You'll do, you say, to them. You'll do, they say, to you. Pudding. A song. It. Sur les monceaux de corps morts, de rocs, de briques, s'ouvrir un large chem. Goes quite. In. Like this. One little spoon. Later. What are you. Says. I don't understand. Well, the hip. Thinking. Egg sounds. Fresh out. You'll do. Try the antipsychotic, says the manager, it's excellent tonight. I'd go for that egg myself. What you're talking about. All you. Says the. My milkshake brings. Egg. I'm scared. An egg. C. All the. Slow fly. I can't have it. Can eat. I'm male spotted crakes. Kill, says the jerboa. To the. De-escalate, says the manager. Scared. It's what they're like. They're like, O moralist, frown not so dark, something, the rapier wit of Prior. Yeah, says the pig, Prior had a rapier wit. Ex. Eggy uvula. Sheds. But Trump's is way rapier. Trump's rapier wit is way rapier than Prior's rapier wit was. I like, it as true as odd is, says the shrew, rhymed with a God or Goddess. And when they stick the ladle in that poor woman, see the Woman's aukward Pain, and get the Ladle out again, that's good. Yeah but come on, says the banausic ostrich. That's nothing. Leave scolding. Egg toe. Laden with formalities. But essentially the same. The Colliquament grows Opace. It for. They. The spotted. Dainties enow. Name the egg. Olf. Crake. Thing that. One eye. Dog. One egg. Dog. Dog. Weigh given. Don't take this the wrong way, says the. Only one way out. Fatted floor. Solwid. Lamb.

I'll be damned, says. I won't be five minutes, says. I'll be, I won't be, there, true, gone. I am staunch. I'd've known. Scraping. Has the chahooblies. At the sounding. I'd've. As steel. For fear of being. Two shakes, says the manager, I'm not eating that. Quick, says the mayfly. To match. The whipworm, bail, whence my inexpugnable consolation. He's hardly touched it. And people are starving. And paying her debts. Skurce any vittles for their stummux, says the eagle-eyed razor clam, and all you lot do, day in, day out, is swan around disintegrating. Animals these days. Tush, says the dog, when the appetite is real. Real, says the pig, and bullish. Anything it seems wears thin. Tread softly, says the ant. Will do to stay the craving. Am I alone, says the abalone, in wearying of this bloodbath of bloviation. Take it from me, says the furtive cabbage white, before anyone sees, in obsessa via pauperi pax est, you're better off emaciated. Outside, says the manager. Dog, says the pig. Yes, says the dog, what is it my pet. Tell me in my ear. I think I want to go now, says the pig. I know, says the dog, it's ok. Head cheese butty, says the manager. What is it now. I really want to go. Do you, why. I don't know. I don't feel right. What would we do. I don't just want to go home, it's too early. And too late. I don't know, I could quite happily crawl into bed now. And when you are there, could you quite happily be there. Alone with me. I don't know, I just want to go. I'm tired. Strange, you've never been tired. Now, all of a sudden, you are tired. You seem like you're having a good time to me. What, him, don't be stupid. Not exactly my type. Fuck off, you love antlers. I don't know what you're talking about, unless you don't. Can this wait. It will have to. Thousands of them will have to die, you do know, and for what, but that can wait. Why are we still here, says the dog. Walk with me. I mean, walk me. Dog, says. Through everything. Pig, yes. Please walk away. My pet. What is it. What's that frown. I wish, says the mole, I was me in the ground. I think I want to go now. Can I come. With, or in, says the pig, quick, pull out. Ok in. Quick pinch my nipples. Fuck. Fuck. Just kidding. With. Not in. What, I said with. Stop it. I'm serious, stop it. Just stop. Stop.

16

Get out of my bunkbed. Over here, says the bream. I think maybe I'll just leave, says the abalone, I know when I'm not welcome. I love that, says the bat. You think you do, says the shrew. You're lonely, says the abalone, and you're welcome to yourself, any time, just pick up the phone. If you know what I mean. I'll be off, says the bat. I'm on the late shift. Early start, says the giant penguin. I can't have a big one. That's just it, says the sky. Big to you is an atom to me, your flood is not even my teardrop. It's, says. We must do this. That's me, says. O pig. Not for me. Not me, not this time. They opened up on us with tanks, drones, and helicopters. The fucking GHF, who do you think. Think about it for a minute. Ciao, says the cow, what now. You forget. For lonc he. Mayfly, the stomach. Which one was it, says the cow, point him out. Ta'ddaset, says. Meaning, says. I've been lentilised, says. Scant this. The green-eyed. Is and leane and his leor deaðlich. Because you tread on my children. Das. Just let. And my children's children. And blac and elheowet. Me. Legal life. Boven. Carking. Leef ick, boven zweef. Prick a man. Ick. In the tongue, in the eye. Look up, you'll. And save his life. See me, waving. Saying. Discontiguating. Try to breathe, says. Excess. Now imagine. Polish. Otherwhiles it gnaweth. Says. Knock knock. And byteth bitterly, if. Knock. I'll be your baby. Mind. You don't shut it. Einer. It's going. The rest. The hippo, good to. Up. Of this baba off, says. Jeden. Whom I omit.

Says. Don't let me keep you, says the manager, yawning. The Lord of hosts shall lop the bough with terror, I forgot. What. I am a terrorist, says God. I'm notorious for terror. There's even a phrase for it, they say, something will put the fear of me into someone. No-one else has the fear of them put into that many millions of children. And I tell you what, they're right. Because I'm a nasty fuck and I don't give a shit about you. Or what happens to me. I'll be dead, if that's what you get off on, I don't care, it's all the same shit. That's why I threw the stones down the sky on to the neighbours of my people, who are also my children, it's because I don't give a shit. Kill 'em all, let one sort 'em out. You call a pineapple that plays the trumpet. Do what. As one gathereth eggs. Says. Tanquam equus. More often, says the dotty locust, and harder, while we're at it. Endlichen. Catch up. O dim vast. Theilmenschheit. Balloon. Hysteron. To be alright, says the. The. Boeuf de mer. O lonely abalone. Wait. Dog. Like a dog. Everybody knew. I'll be. Who's. Dead. To say. Pop goes. There. The hippo. There. For me. But soon. The least you. Anyway, says the. And did. Cyclian psychobabble, says. Nothing. The phoney. O manager. Abalone, bobbing along at. Agammaglobulinemic. The ear only. Darts. Convulsed. Through the ear. At the bottom. Are you still. Lady, says. Serving. Run. I'll be. Says. O. O. Home. O. Made flesh. For it. Sorry. Of the beautiful. You just. Briny. O. Missed last. Everyone back. Orders. To mine, says. Says the. Sea. Camel. Ant. Sky. Whipworm. Flywheel. Manager.

17

Nobody is saying that, says. I never fucked her, categorically. Bivore. Haunc. Auoir esté. The night is young and hot. False. Enter. En fin. Bâtards, screams. Says. I forget. But these frendes wylle neuer forget. Johnnie Moore and the devil. At it. Everyone form a chiliagon, says the pig. Done sone. Get. Stemme this cyon, don't you. I love this song. Iron on my face, says the conger eel, if it's not the tight-ass. Boys will. Transmuée. Quoll, don't ask. The. The usual. Hell out of here. Me for. Isn't that him, says. Duck. Don't. Money. A nerve. Say agayne. Voila. That's it, poke him. My face is on. Your. Fire, says. Be boys. En. God codepninge. Ferrero. The trippy. Buzzard. Rocher. Rochier. Categorically false. Johnnie Moore. Lord. Lard. Lardlord. The company a-gaping. Bosys. Fields. Flies. I never met herbivore. Johnnie. Who sang. Johnny. Devilled. Mulford. This. Bon. Song, says the. Cyon, don't you thin. Pig. Good dog. Fuck out. Manager. Manager. Can I. Nine. The devil. Get a room. Children everywhere. Don't let him steal your heart away. Lager. The. Who is then most busie. Form. En fin. Even think. Trippy. A-gasping. Neuer forget. Love this song. My face is on fire. Isn't that. Buzzard. Boys will. Johnnie Moore. Stemme this cyon. Be. The pig. Manager. Everyone form a chiliagon. Says the sky, en fin transmuée, you messed with the wrong sky. Bye. I don't think. Buzzardscreen. About you. Diriguisse malis. I pull a ponytail of spinach out of my eyeball. Johnnie. Put it

in. Let me. Words. Be boys. Lager. Form. En fin. The
unserious one, which is even better. Moore is the.
Imagine having to. Who sang this. Fields. Devil. Out
of my way. Go away, says the hippo, nine. Suckle his.
Neuer forget. Sick kid. I never met herbivore. Not
today, says. You've got to be. This sky is. Joking. Left.
Bye. Trippy. Over. Everyone form. From yesterday.
The sky. And that sky wasn't there the day before.

18

Don't try me, says the plucky sprat, I've been left out overnight. Get the brush. A pig. Overnight. Pig. A pig after my own heart. For our part, says the halibut, let us content ourselves. Yonder's a sow lies grubbing. Says the. With. Spiral. Noting the BATM dip. Oh yeah. Barmy bunyip. Where have you. Wound foam. Been all my, says the pig. Batching. Pig. Don't. Life. Such chopping. Hurl. Ask, says. Me at the foot of your throne and bid me dine on dust, says the manager, if it's. Says the. Not my friend. Cheare. Happy. Meet. Halibut. The holybut, what'll it. Is he, says the cuddly hologram, for. Be. Whom. Anyone for a prelibation of our happiness, says the dog, no time, sorry. It's a bit. This, I say, to a considerative. Late for that, says. Like the present. In the sag bend. Mind. If she who. The pigges. Gone off. Some. Head speakes it. Says. Care of the Vineyard of. The hairy. Truth, shall lye pigging. De Pig. Eel. Prior to time. Noribus, says the yak, remember that. Pignore pluribus. Ha, yeah. I'm a pig. You would be. The bat. Potior. Mole tempura. Best in town, says the manager. Est in. Stefanik. Lait brûlée for. Cremabit. Me please. Spoon, says the stick. Bread. Insect, feed. Addictos, says Cyprian, says the baboon, don't. Last. Forget, with living flames, if you can believe that. May be flesh. Omni pig. Pig. Nore prior tempore. Crackling. Biblical. Superior to any the other. Of your own farrow, says the pig, you can talk. Creatures. On. Are capable of. Vit, says. Old pigs.

Prefer 'fore pettitoes. Pow'r. The pig. Grunt. Pick. Of the pig train. To. BATM dip. Stiffen into stone. Glycol. Dans le brouillard où rien. Happy. N'a. One. Hour. Plus. Just. The curse of others drowns. De forme, you. Ended. My voice, says the. Voice. I'm afraid. Pigging. Says the. I'm. Know how. Opaque third. Halibut. Party. Hell. Operations. Manager. It ends. Local. It goes. Is when you have felt an organic. Hell is. Unity. Without saying. Dying for a leak, says. Folded up in the napkin of incogitancy and sloth again, I see, says the stygichthys. When are you going to get out of the deep, dark. Du. Happy is he. Côté. Says. Du. The macaque, for. Hen. Night of superstition. It. Pourceau la. Like scraping. You must be. Balance. Whom. Joking. It. The halibut. Says. And inhibition. Is. The pig. The hours of hope. I just. That are. Ran all. The most. Broacht. The way. Numerous. Here. Here we are. Here. Here you go. Here you are, says the civet.

19

You know what, says the binturong. Let's not, says the dog, if it's all the same. As if we didn't have a better idea. Hit me, says the jellyfish. Only out of a cavilling disposition, says the rooster, are we still here, saying anything, at all. Incredible, says the frantic moose, you've only been here five minutes. Thanks, says the manager, but no thanks, thank you, that'll do, thank you. Leave time for later. When you're ready, says the bear, in your dreams. Let's hear it, says the Galápagos pink land iguana, and let's not be always licentious in gazing after vanities, or always true to ourselves in harkening after lies. Thanks, says the dog. Everyone shut up. I tell you what. Don't listen to me. I love it when you beg, says the lamb. You'll pay for this, says the mayfly, genocide, in instalments. Spread the cost. One good, honest pint of wort, says the deceptively large sponge, whenever you've put your clothes on and unknotted your hands. Shh, says the screech owl, it's starting. Switch your phone off. Thanks, says the dog. So, I think we all probably feel. I know I do, says the sheltopusik. I wasn't, says the manager, I was going to lick his face. Or is that not allowed now. It means I'm happy. What I'm saying, says the dog, thank you, is, I think we probably all feel, right now, and I'm not pointing fingers, but maybe we should, like we do owe it, to ourselves, as fellow beings, all doing our best, all sentient, to do something. Now we all know that Palestine Action has been proscribed, together with the Maniacs Murder Cult, nobody is saying we want to get into all of that. Nobody is saying we should give back their strip of land, or anything, but surely it's not asking much to tell them we know it's theirs, and to have some kind of formula to recite at the start of events, a sort of purely verbal restitution, that thanks them for being a good host and acknowledges that they never ceded anything, and doesn't do our credibility on the left any harm, either, and it probably needs to be in the first minute or so, in case some asshole has a fit and walks out, essentially, and people do, we don't want them to be able to say they didn't hear us do it, we being many, for conscience sake. What are you saying, says the tortoise, that we should get in trouble with the police. Don't be stupid, says the dog. We all have somewhere to be. I think I see where this is headed, says the chicken. Anyway, I'm not really talking about that, says the dog. What I'm saying is, since the right to protest is the cornerstone of our democracy, does it not behove us to find a way to express what we're feeling, without causing criminal damage, which has no place in legitimate protests. You read my mind, says the salp, was it any good. I didn't finish it, honestly, says the Nooitgedachter, I only just set fire to it. What about Palestine Inaction, says the chicken. You don't mince, says the tardigrade, your words, why then do you mince your principles. Thank you, says the dog. I love it, says the lamb. Anagram of penitential casino, says the gibbering sild. Oh yeah, says the heart urchin, nationalise pectin too. I mean, we're going to die soon anyway. Palestine Inaction, says the chamois, it could work. Actaeon, Leninist PI, says the church mouse. What about Palestine Talk, says the baboon. I'll add that to the tombola, says the dog. Any anagrams, says the chicken. Antlike petals, natal spikelet, AI tank pellets, AKA Epstein LLT, we're laughing. I like Palestine Inaction better, says the moth. Punchy, says the slug. I know, says the dog, that some of us have a lot on our plate. Some of us, says the stork, would kill for a plate. Not all plates are the same size, says the crow. I just think we're not doing everything we possibly can. He's got a point, says the swordfish. So do I, says the baboon. You do know, that plane they damaged with paint at Brize Norton, not only was it clearly displaying the union jack, but it had been used to transport members of the Royal family to engagements, like the Lolita Express, says the prawn. Watch your mouth, says the manager, it starts slow but picks up and eventually gets quite engrossing. Not everyone has someone to wash their plate up for them, says the Batak. We don't have to lie down, chained up, in doorways, do we, says the sheltopusik, like homeless people, I'm afraid. Some people are not homeless, says the rabbit, through no fault of their own. No, says the dog. We weren't all born, says the mink, with a silver spoon stuck in our eye. We don't have to swan about like we think we're the Dedan Kimathi, or Perpetua and Felicity, of humanity, do we, says the gorilla. No, says the dog. Leave that to them. I hope they don't commit suicide. I tell you what, says the ocelot, there are plenty of decent people out there who aren't ashamed. I'm not going to keep my mouth shut, says the horse. This has gone on for long enough. I just think it's time those of us who don't have an axe to grind found our voices, says the chicken. And spoke up, says the termite, it doesn't matter who we voted for. This brain fluid has got a hair in it, says the sponge. Don't look at me, says the manager, it grew on me. What did I miss, says the pig,

I've been here for years. Finally, says the Argentine black and white tegu. Before you start snorting turmoilously, says the capybara, and can scarce forbear to sneer, there is no political convenience in what we are seeking to do today. Quite, says the blesbok. I can't wait, says the peafowl, if there is no time. Make do, says the ferret. Don't make me laugh, says the beaver, since when was this a democracy. I think we're getting off topic, says the dog, hand these round. Wow, says the tick, I seriously was not expecting this. I like what you've done with the name, says the quebracho crested tinamou. Thanks, says the dog. Palestine Inaction, says the wallaroo, in the house. Fuck it, says the hippo, I'm in. There's really no point, says the dog, at this stage, obfusticating, we've seen what good that did. They bloody ignored us, says the duck. Less hassle to let us blow off some steam, says the dassie, no doubt. Jesus, says the seal, I never thought of that. I know how they think, says the eel, they always think, sooner or later, we'll get bored, and go home. They can kiss my ass, says the koala. How come, says the wombat. You never let me. You're too rough, says the koala. They know what they're doing. They'd never dream, says the insecure Reeves's pheasant, of understanding we too are capable of being clear-eyed about the broader threat landscape. They're in for a surprise, says the mule. What will we tell our kids, says the goat, when they look us in the eye and ask what we did, oh nothing, it was very complicated. I'm not going to stand here, says the brown anole, and pretend I have all the answers. Viva Palestine Inaction, says the drunk badger. Yes we can, says the flea. It's about more than just Palestine, says the dove. Bring it on, says the giant aardvark. Read my lips, says the earwig, no dead children. We've got this, says the antelope. All power, says the Essex skipper, to Palestine Inaction. Can we leave power out of it, says the turkey, for a change. Get peace done, says the boorish fawn. De-escalation is not a dinner party, frankly, says the pika, there are no designated drivers. Peace, says the chub. Palestine Inaction, Palestine Inaction, come on, say it with me, says the crapulous, limpid, dowdy, trenchant squid. If any here should attempt to deny the goodness of our cause, and betray our friends, to the hazard of their equanimity, may they be ashamed, says the tenrec. Out, says the manager. Palestine Inaction, says the giant aardvark, is not about burying your head in the sand, if you can find it, while the defenceless are butchered in holding pens. Revenues from the US arm of MBDA debouch merrily into Hertfordshire, says the culpeo, right into the back pocket of BAE Systems, in front of our watering eyes. I don't know about you, says the chicken, but I refuse to be infamous for all posterity. I'm not scared, says the monito del monte, of the consequences of doing what's right, come what may, I'm only scared of who I'd become if I did nothing. There is a tribunal, says the pit pony, higher than any administered by HM Courts and Tribunals Service, last time I checked, I will answer for myself only at that. That will be exciting, says the manager. They can't arrest us all, says the herring.

20

I hate how you always take me here. You don't care that I'm allergic, if I am. It's all about you, you say. It's all about you, more like, you say, it was always all about you. You pig, says the pig. Swanning around, says the dog. Mousehead. Say what you like. What do you say, you say. Say thank you. Thank you. Finally. Don't thank me thank Netanyahu. You know what I'm talking about. You don't have to say anything. Anything you do say may not actually be something you say, anyway. You don't grow up by thinking Satan is real, shit, I better join the Satanists, before it's full up. You grow up by thinking, Satan is not real, and the Satanists can get along fine without me. Like everyone else. So when, one day, right when you're spreadeagled on a mountaintop, exulting, asking nothing of the herd but that it get its act together and fasten fetters upon the thousand necks of this beast, foretasting the überkranich, the real Netanyahu shows up, in a nimbus of sulphur, cackling, all you can do is think, was I right not to become a Satanist. As if that has anything to do with anything, says the cow, eyes on the prize. You were misled by sylphs. Ask me if you don't believe me. What, the same one who gives you pins and needles, liver problems, and a virtual abdominal aortic aneurysm the moment you open your mouth, yeah, thanks, I'll pass. I never asked for a mouth that opens. Because, I'm telling you, right now, with all this going on, if I was a Satanist, and the actual real Netanyahu showed up, maybe he'd have been willing to listen. He could have been your patron, says the mole, like Nero, and helped you get your allegories up the algorithm. You have to be prepared to give and take. I'd have sucked that asshole so hard his tailbone'd've harpooned my throat in, says the walrus, for a taste of celebrity in the wide world of letters. I'm sick of banging my head against this ceiling fan, importuning it to get it over with, for once, and decapitate me, so that my work can outlive me and assume its destined rung on the skyey career ladder hereinabove hacked up and incinerated in principled seclusion. And if he'd screamed stop what the fuck are you doing have you lost your mind, I'd have stopped. Why are we here, says the wild ass. He never meant shit to me. It's for the best, says the bos mutus. I blame myself. When it's not my fault. Exactly. It did its best. The fact is everyone got distracted. The sun, says the pernickety cormorant, defying its higher-ups, may have got in their eyes, if you know what I literally mean. Every night when they're asleep in their beds the sun may have caved the roof in, like a head, burned down the ceiling, thrown the fan out, laid down next to them, gently blown on their eyelids, given them a pat, and strode right in through the lens. I still love you. I just don't know who I mean. You weren't in the mood. Thank fuck, says the cow, that was a close shave, I hate the mood. We cows have the mood like you have the spoken. Don't ask me what I think about mood word. You think spoken word is bad, try being forcefully inseminated, locked up in a filthy, overcrowded shed, where you can't graze, or lie down, and made to stand through an evening of funny anecdotes, hammy idpol doggerel, love, and being you, and you can't even get stoned, because the entire stockpile was used up by God on the fleeing

Amorites in the going down to Bethhoron. I'll say this for Satan, says the manager, he got around a bit. Nobody knew how long it would last. Days would go by and you'd start to wonder. When you're in the mood, like that, really deep, for what feels like an eternity, and you never even think about not being in the mood, being in the mood starts to become more important than what you do. The truth is, says the brill, you have to admit, he was never going to kill all of them. He'd kill enough to make you think, no way, he's actually going to do it. Satan wasn't above the odd dubious jibe, says the jerboa. He didn't mean it. More children were murdered in front of their mothers by the GHF tonight, says the terrapin. The less deceived, the better.

21

If we search into the cause of laughter, we shall find it partly in the pleasure we take in discovering our own quickness of apprehension, is what it says here, says the sponge, but this is from ages ago. I couldn't tell you what they're saying now. Life is too short, says the stone. In the grand scheme of things, says the pocket mouse, what does it really boot us to bang on about peremptory norms. Efforts fall tragically short, says the spoonbill. There are no disasters, says the banana slug, only opportunities. Let us groan, says the praying mantis. Ninety-two shot dead at the Zikim crossing yesterday, by the way, says the bird of paradise, while I remember. You learn something every day. I'll stick them on your tab, says the manager. You know it, says the crab. Sometimes my heart hath been full of deadness, says the rock monitor, and uncomfortableness. Shut up, did you know, says the rooster, that in his original definition of genocide, arrived at by a thorough historical study of the laws and practices of the Nazis in Germany and in the territories they occupied, Lemkin said that one way genocide is effected is, and I quote, by substituting vocational education for education in the liberal arts, in order to prevent humanistic thinking. That was then, says the dog. Cheer up, says the pig, it might never happen. What else is in there, says the Yangtze finless porpoise. In Lemkin's list, says the rooster, oh, tons of things, introducing a starvation rationing system, lowering of the survival capacity of children born of underfed parents, mass killings, you name it. I, for one, says the kangaroo, will not. Yeah, but come on, says the cockroach, how many times do we have to go over this, it only applies if you lose. The GHF is the whole point of genocide. Not the whole point, says the tapeworm, don't exaggerate. As an average man who voted for Trump because we're not going to stand for zombies molesting our babies and who doesn't love a tax cut would say, says the pig, the bear case is real but on a risk-adjusted basis it's an extremely safe bet. I'm all ears, says the manager, genocide or no genocide. Put them away, says the koala, people are listening to themselves trying to eat. Later. Not oversharing, sharing, says the bear. What, says the mare. He said oversharing, says the bear. I think he was talking about something else. No shit, who isn't. It. What. Sentences. Do you call. Don't. I. A man. Without number. Mind me. Can't. Who cheers. Not this again. Now you're asking, says the. Who's asking, says the rat. Diverge drastically. I'm probably talking. Cockroach. From their. Shake this. Yeah. Isn't it. Mmm. The day with insight that brings health. Overall pattern of associations, too. Out. Stomach bug. Something about meaning. And sweetness. Of my pneumostome. Says the cow, how. And shared collateral. To all. Didn't the natives end up getting boiled in head cheese, says the rabbit. Gross, says the slug. Information. Am I meant. Says the banana slug. Thought and work. I think, says. Ninety-two, says the manager, it all adds up. Says the kodkod. God. Phew. To think in this racket. Like this. I don't know, says the abyss, what. I don't know, says the long-eared. I don't know, how. A poet, says the kodkod. What do you mean, says the skink. Funny how. Stop and think. You do it. I don't know. Freak pipistrelle. Says. Odd that. Yourself. The gnat.

How can it. Says. Be. I. What. I don't know. Have you not been listening, says the numbat, they just told you. What. When, says. I don't. The besieged enclave. Oh for. What anyone is. Don't. Can. Fuck's. I was miles. Where. Care. Witness. Whose. I don't know. Sake. Away, says. Meant to do. Join the queue, says the manager. Bone saw, do. Hod. The gnat. You. Odd that. Think that is. Think. They. I'm not. Parked outside. Says. Ok. Says. The sky. Into. The kodkod, repeating myself. I'm not repeating myself, says God, not after last time. I'm not telling you again. Me neither, says the kodkod, thin muth is betuned. He's had. I don't want to have to tell. Listen. You again. To yourselves, says the pig, twice. One at a time, says the manager, or you'll get your claws crushed in the turnstile. One too many, says the springtail, one day. One litter. One nation. Up to some convenient limit or modulus. Got it, says the bedbug. Of all the human. Onegotene. Hogwash, this takes. One each. The Ox. The Carnilove. A hug. Pheasant bar. Oone a-cordyd. Ontogens. Nugget. Wellaway, says the dog, anyone would think. One in one. This was a real head. Out, says the manager. Once the don't knows are excluded, says the bedbug, 11% of the British public think they haven't gone far enough.

22

J'aymasse mieulx estre joieux, says the chipper mudskipper, pass it under the table. Crop. Leave me. Me. How. Some, says. Did you make it out. The beewolf. Lo. Lentils. Not again, says the shrew. Cataphonic identity, says the. Crops stop. Rainbow. I've done this before. Front. Now. Trout, takes a bit. D'un. Of get up and go. You're a barrel of laughs this evening, says the rabbit, what's next, a cento of plosives on the suffocation of a heartbroken foetus, Rabelais in Babylon, roasting God, Columbus at Valladolid, Waleed the wantsum woodworm goes completely wankel in a briquette of charcoal, did it hurt. What precedeth of this mad outrage, says the walrus, is fine by me. Oomph, says the auk, pork is off. What's the fish. Pick your words, says the flea, carefully. Think very carefully before you say anything. Demure lemur. If you want my advice. Dans lentille. Don't. Y a-t-il. Me finish. Fysshmangercrafte. Hundysfishskyn. No way. Let. Is. Fishwife. Real. Fingers. Go free, What the, says the. For once, says the. Manager. Rainbow, hell. Keep it. Identité. In your pants. Like everyone. Trout. For leather. Else. Conteyned. It. Happened here, I only just mopped. In þe oon pond. Elbow. Harske. Sorry. As a. Fishpound. It was an accident. Bloody. Let. Epilinguistic. Boeuf creuse. Time. Hell. For my little. How did you get past. Sorry. Me help. Say, says. I heart. Hunde-fisch. No you're alright, it's fine. The attack on. What are we up to, says the chatrynge pye, how many now. It strikes me that. People should be. A breath of fresh air. Synchronized. My hearts leap up, says the hagfish. Schrafysch. Me do that. Nor money, I looked everywhere. As. Wrote, in the True Levellers' Standard Advanced. And on different bits. Says the fruity rooster. What did. Time in shatters leaves. The beaver. What did. He. Ou. Mean. Non. Say to the langoustine. Well, says the rooster, break in pieces. I. Quickly the bond. Fishpond. Says the bed. Don't know, says the. Of particular property, and disown. Kill. Bug. The music. Bat. This. Bat. Oppressing murder. Bug. Only because you've got claws so big they have their own zip code. Not hinder. I'm gourmet, you're the one who gnaws on sticks for fun. Mother. Was þe hyde of þat hulke hally al. But. Ouer. But. Langoustique. Beaverteen. Stop shit. Let. Happening. Nature's. I tell you. This craze. Stirring, says the spoonbill. For the jeu phonique. For time. This was then. Ladies. Needs. Ans am ieu lo chant el ris. We may be from different worlds. Her balls in a cream-colour'd beaver. In its decrescendo. Langoure and dole. Duo. Shok de platfysshe. Fifty-one. From giving. Un. The tank, says the fish. On the sill. Swerdfyche. Her children suck. Still. Dead. Sillon. Profonde erreur, says the. Prof. Raring. Door. Swa swa. Ondir. Fugl. Me out. Please, please. Oðð e.

23

I support Palestine Action. J'. Says. AI a, se, se zn, a sane size. The potty-mouthed stickleback. En ai assez d'entendre. Learn to read. Puis trop placet antinoise. A Nazi sees. Didn't bat. Says the bot. I support Palestine Action, considered as. Brailler, says. Openeth. Discourse-initial in the speakable locutionary, says the. A. An eye. Litel. Jangly leech, speech act with felicity conditions only. I support Latina potencies. Says. In broken Ngapak-Ngapak. The windhover. I sup. Lentils, grass. Blood. One down. Time of the end is at. Port. Pecan tonalities. Arrest me, says, if. Discretliche þe eyen, or I'll rip them. Open borders. Open. I support open at inelastic. Psst. En plein vent. I sport up Atlantic peonies. I support Palestine Action. You like it when I talk. Say it loud. Says the ticklish. O antiseptical one PPS U R TI. Stick. Limbs. Insect, gimme a pat. Put it there. Inanest poetical I. Support your local. Seventh trumpet. Borderline shepherd. Une sorte de tromperie fondamentale, says the mental earth. Of his fathers. Behold. Here it. Worm, in facts. They speak for themselves. In fact. Atonic tapelines I support. Capitalise on ten I support. Anticipates Leno I SPT. Pour. Yvette's y végéter et y. LOL. Heed. Mourir inutiles. Screamy little inch. Preserveth man and beast. Act on alien spite. I support that. When, says the reticulated giraffe, crafty enemies surrounded us, and our heaven was looking overcast, with clouds and thick darkness resting upon us, and a sea of miseries breaking in, the Lord in the multitude of his tender mercies hath seasonably appear'd for us, ancient, spoliate, and broke the snare that we might get away, I think you know what I mean. I don't believe I need to spell it out. Le bavardage humain. I don't think anyone is under any illusions.

Look, says the pig. Engulf. If. Of. Anyone. Mi. Is. Hit meme. Having second thoughts. First. Serewe þou makest newe. Say now. Stock levels, macro. Says the. Or. Of. Regulatory. Can we get back on. Look. Headwinds. Topic, please, now, please. Says. Du côté du. On a GAAP basis. Boa constricteur la balance. Potted ants. Early mover's. Pencha. Bite me, too. When these whan þese words I woordes I. Not in the face, dear ear. Starmer called the move wrong. Lick my knee-ear, says. I hearde, thouhty I bicom. The ditzy cricket. Done, says the hippo. Advantage. Hippo. At a CAGR. Sweet hope. O. If that. Jog on egg. And sour. Hard, says the. Ne. Eel, to believe. No rage ne tecche of woodshipe, bodies all over. That's bodies for you. The place. Don't trip. Focus. Armchair starvation. Armchair bruit tout. Before they could get their tongues all. Says. Look out. Kanst. The myotonic Tennessee. If. Fainting. Only you. Goat, scrimpingly made flesh. Quod. Says the. Please. She, þe song. Don't. Ox. Please. Oh go on then, says the Dinilysia, shut the. Window. Fuck up. On Gibeon's bloody plain, da. Music. Dum. Forbearance. Quand les boeufs vont deux a deux le labourage en va mieux. Man, says the mole, that's. Da. Þat Israel of Daan song. Data mine. I. I have a horse in this. Sex. Race. Class. Fiat Daan. The man. Coluber in via I am. D'appetisante faim. Farm me. Þe horned and Daan. Do. Says the pig. Get the manager. Þe crookede. Step on it. In the neck. Bite folk. Fort.

Dangdut. Debt farm. Fawning corn. In stelth I wole.
Snake. Pig. Veritable. Like. Dete. In the head. Go all
go al. Da. Sexy. Racy. Classy. Stilleliche. Of 37%.
And bihynde. Blinded. And 6. Bite þe. Hard to
know. By the look of it. Nails. 3%. As nails.

All options are on the table, says the pig, but look at the table. You've got to be joking, says the yak, do you think I'm made of flour. I don't think you're made of anything, says the louse, if anything, I think you're made up. Aren't we all. No, says the dog. I'd better not catch you smoking, says the manager, unless you're on fire. Hello, who's this, he's adorable. Who's a chinny varlot. That's right, says the vulture, let it all. Absquotulate, says the manager, before I autopsychographize. Out. Your mother, says the lark. I'd leave now if I could, says the seal, because there is no way out. 'Tis bawled about streets lowder than naughty turneps, says the chinchilla, nobody can get out. I have a great mind to be saucy, says the lamb, if I put my drippings to it. Where am I. I'll tell you, says the do-goody bandicoot, if you stand me a bucket of surgical staples and a tub of elastic bands. I'll be hang'd then, and now I am to look too, says the nuthatch, show me the door. There isn't one, says the seal. We haven't got one. We can tunnel out, says the unflappable umbrellabird, with our heads. Are you high, says the skate. Yes, says the unanswering umbrellabird. So am I, says the sky. I used to love it. Don't point. So the likes of you can't reach up and poke me, I hate being touched. Anyway the IDF filled them in with sponge bombs. Shrive me, says the Lord Derby's eland, you crude, shriveldy, duftberauscht barrel of darkness, or I'll gore your forehead, shackle it to a metal bed frame, and end up having to amputate it at the knee, bring that ass over here. Coming, says the ass. I want to go home, too, says the chicken, it's so loud. I'd give anything, says the ass, to say that, but some comedian has apparently stapled my jaws together. I can't hear you. You can't handle the door, says the lamb. More of the same. Oak nouȝt me to gydere, says the root-mouthed jellyfish, with the long-eared owl, I am frightened of what it will say. Have you eaten, says the floor. Nothing, says the mayfly, for days. Tranche auditive. Give what you can. Are you alone, says the bed. Now there's a question. What am I going to do with you. Ask me, says the question. I just did. I said, what am I going to do with you. Ask me again, says the question. Can you be anything I want. Yes, says the question, anything, so long as it's a real thing. How do I ask you it. The same way you'd ask anything else it, says the question. What if there isn't anything else. What if this is it. What if there's nothing you can do. And that's it. You only had to ask, says the question, says the dog, it was me saying it. All along. Could it have stopped then. No, says the question. Then why ask. Well, says the question, because it is always good to ask, and always good to be questioning. No question, says the answer. Now let me ask you something. Ask away, says the question. No, I will ask here. Ask me, says the question, who I am. I asked first. The question, says the question, in question, is not how a genocide could happen, here, in 2025, while Trump claps, and rapes the sky, after all, he is its chief financer, you can't blame him for feeling a bit like a proud dad making an effort at the school play, we all know the answer to that. The question is, what. Not, says the dog. Bere ȝe no ȝok. Now, now. Wiþ folk of fals bileue. Is not the time. If you don't want

your head caved in like a tunnel. It's no use, says
the hippo, we shouldn't joke about it. Nobody is
laughing. Not here. I'm not here, says the nuthatch,
can I go. Look, a fly, says the dog. If I keep my head
down and don't say anything or look at anybody,
then is there a way out. There's no way out, says the
sky. Do I look like an emergency exit.

26

E ce a molt grauntz tortz. I dream of bellies. What for, says the manager. Consiliis non futtilis auctor. I don't understand. I don't know why I come here, what am I doing here. Yet, says the dog. From futtile, says the pig, lato ore, fundo angusto. Don't let any of it get on my plastic sheets, says the manager. What are you scared of, and waiting for, here, with no way out, why aren't you over there, with them, going out. Is evil even real, says the dog, if not, why not. Look, says the manager. Rem nulli obscuram. Mais qui donc tient la chaîne, says the pig. Aren't you tired, do you not want to go home. That might work, says the dog. There are times when it is futile, says the pig, to sustain life, many since Quinlan. I don't see a way back. Yet nothing is dark, yet, says the manager. Nothing is obscure. Everyone can see. And us, says the dog. What you mean. There is that. Can I do anything, says the pig, I like, if it feels right. How does it feel, though. Recanalization, says the manager, itself, is futile sometimes. A long vessel holds good things. Thus the mind, having heard, holds good, pours and drinks. It can't be. It is, says the manager, there's no point of no return. Cuncti se scire fatentur, ask anyone you like. But sometimes I don't like anyone, says the pig. How could they, what got into them. A futile vessel holds good things, and a sincere vessel holds good things, says the manager. Yeah but look at them. Why are they not even empty. I don't know, says the dog.

Why. There's more, says the manager. There always is. Do you mean, says the dog. Yes. But how. What do you do when it's not thin enough. Tac an homur ant bet hit. There it is. They're not stupid, they'll get the message.

27

Don't look at me. I hit meme stock levels in my sleep. Durelease shithousery. Early days. More of less. Schon schwebt der Geist des Känguruh. Where did everybody go. Where it hurts. Speak of the device. Lest. Reconnoitring ironies, may not that be that scintilla today that blows up into the sun tomorrow. I like the odd wall. I make believe they fold like blinds. Loopy, scatty, disincarnated. For to carry me home when I'm out of it, and take advantage. If that. Desconseillatz. Roll on reality. Hard to know. Ahead of ourselves. See. Grow. Focus. Before they go. Full-blown brains. Look out. Ans Ende kommet das Korn. What you quod. Only you. In þe song. Unblisse cumath. Ox, trill. Nitidity. Fainting. Please me. Shut the window. Fuck up. Music off. Cui bono, light of it, or hollow trunk or probe. Borrowed shadow. Something gives back. Not all men. Owe it. Human touch. Clean slate. Skyway. Open architecture for end-user integrations, reliable situational awareness where it is most needed. Gap'd wide and foam'd. Outputs. Joking apart. From the heart. Falling for fear. Liggeth the bon stil novo. Not long. Alaska fiasco. Comms. All in one. Gaspant, air-fried. One mind down. How I feel about that. In lieu. Good to be true. And you. Good to know. And dreamless. This. Unheiȝthe beoth the sidwowes, still too high. So nigh. Think the world. And yet. And China pinks. An eyebrow. And so small eaters. Fagz valens. Mind your mind. Have I gone yet. And the rank mist. Make

no gloose. If I reach. Please to lengthen. Taryeth
no animal. Out of my hand. Minus one. Pettish,
cornered, manly, di pace. Stay far. Ja da und nicht
dort. On fumish stomachs. Waving them past.

Published by The Last Books, Amsterdam
www.thelastbooks.org

Designed and typeset by Phil Baber

Printed in the Netherlands by Wilco

ISBN 978-94-91780-93-6